THOMAS MERTON
THE DEVELOPMENT
OF A
SPIRITUAL
THEOLOGIAN

Donald Grayston

Toronto Studies in Theology
Volume 20

The Edwin Mellen Press
New York and Toronto

Library of Congress Cataloging In Publication Data

Grayston, Donald.
  Thomas Merton, the development of a spiritual
theologian.
   Bibliography: p.
   1. Merton, Thomas, 1915-1968. 2. Trappists--
United States--Biography. 3. Spirituality--Catholic
Church--History of doctrines--20th century.
4. Catholic Church--Doctrines--History--20th century.
I. Title.
BX4705.M542G7 1984   248'.092'4 [B]   84-27299
ISBN 0-88946-758-7

Toronto Studies in Theology
Series ISBN 0-88946-975-X

All rights reserved. For more information contact:
The Edwin Mellen Press
P.O. Box 450
Lewiston, New York 14092

Printed in the United States of America

For Ginger

CONTENTS

INTRODUCTION

It was only in the second half of the fifties that Thomas Merton realized or accepted the fact that he was a figure of literary and historical interest. After that, he probably became a little more careful as regards his writing, at least in relation to projects for publication. (Some of his letters and his unpublished journal, "A Vow of Conversation," however, supply evidence that the not-for-publication Merton could be just as revealing and artless as the pre-literary-figure Merton.) Thus a large part of the interest of this present book comes from the small ways in which the incompletely-reconstructed young monk expressed his growing edges and his sore points, his struggles to grow.

Certainly Seeds of Contemplation and New Seeds of Contemplation--considered as one organic whole--provide the best textual entrée into this growth-process. The textual basis for this book is the variorum edition of the five existing documents/versions of Seeds and New Seeds published as Thomas Merton's Rewriting: The Five Versions of Seeds/New Seeds of Contemplation as a Key to the Development of his Thought (Toronto, Ontario, and Lewiston, New York: The Edwin Mellen Press, 1985). On the basis of the variorum, I have tried to set out some of the major shifts in his development as person and theologian between 1948 and 1961 as those shifts are textually evidenced in the four successor documents to the original typescript. That Merton developed during this period is widely appreciated: my contribution here is a study of this self-critical development within a self-limiting portion of his voluminous writings.

Probably it will be useful to the prospective reader
to say here that my work does not duplicate the fine
piece of sleuthing presented in William H. Shannon's
Thomas Merton's Dark Path: The Inner Experience of a
Contemplative (New York: Farrar, Straus and Giroux, 1981;
rpt. New York: Penguin Books, 1982). Shannon does include
expository chapters on the first edition of Seeds and on
New Seeds as part of his survey of Merton's writing on
contemplation. But the real center of interest in his book
is the exploration in Chapters 4 and 5 of Merton's unpublished work, The Inner Experience, and the structural
laying-open in Chapter 7 of The Climate of Monastic
Prayer, more widely circulated as Contemplative Prayer
(New York: Herder, 1969; rpt. Garden City, NY: Doubleday,
1971).

This book also had an earlier form, as part of my
doctoral dissertation presented to the University of St
Michael's College, Toronto, in 1980. For this publication,
I have brought my reading of the secondary literature on
Merton up to date, and have made a number of additions
and corrections in the text and notes as a result. In
my own writing I have tried to be as inclusive as possible: but I have left the quotations from Merton in
their pre-inclusive state, inasmuch as to do otherwise
would only have led to artificiality and complication,
as well as a separation from the period of their origin.

I am grateful that the appearance of this book gives
me an opportunity in print to thank those persons who have
been instrumental in helping me in my studies of Merton.
First among these is Herbert Richardson, dissertation
advisor, mentor and friend. I am deeply grateful also to

Sr Thérèse Lentfoehr, who died in 1981, for lending me the typescripts of <u>Seeds</u> and <u>New Seeds</u>, without which act of trust the writing of the dissertation would not have been possible. Thanks also go to Patrick Hart, Merton's sometime secretary, for his gracious encourage- ment from the time of my first letter to him in 1972; to Robert Daggy, Curator of the Thomas Merton Studies Center at Bellarmine College in Louisville, and Chief of Research for the Merton Legacy Trust, for his warm welcome to the Center and his valuable assistance in many ways; to Joanne McWilliam Dewart, who introduced me to the serious study of Merton; to Michael Higgins, Director of the St Jerome's Centre for Catholic Experi- ence in Waterloo, Ontario, for friendship and the joy of co-operation in many projects related to Merton; to my parents for their unfailing confidence and support, and most of all to my wife and children for their acceptance of many inconveniences during the years that this book has been a-borning.

Particular thanks go also to my parish, the Christ- ian Community of All Saints, in Burnaby, British Columbia, for the study leave in 1979 which enabled me to finish the first draft of the dissertation, and for the sabba- tical leave which I am presently enjoying. Together with these go my thanks to the faculty of the Episcopal Divi- nity School in Cambridge, Massachusetts, for granting me a Procter Fellowship and thereby the opportunity during my sabbatical to make use of the resources of this fine school. Special thanks go to Prof. E. V. N. Goetchius of EDS for his particular kindness in making available to me a congenial space in which to work. I acknowledge also, most sincerely and gratefully, the financial sup- port for the sabbatical from my parish and diocese, from the H. R. MacMillan Fund administered by the Vancouver School of Theology, from the General Synod of the Anglican Church of Canada and from the Canadian Council of Churches.

*

"Daddy, who is Thomas Merton, and why do you talk about him so much?" Thus Megan Grayston, then aged eight, one night at the supper table.

As to the first part of the question, I hope that the book gives sufficient information and interpretation. As to the second: it is because I am one of those many who feels that Merton was writing to him very personally, but not individually; it is because Merton deals in his writings with the most critical aspects of contemporary society--the recovery of the contemplative attitude in an activist world, peace and nonviolence, and the encounter of the great religions in a shrinking world; and it is because he offers to all persons of faith and all persons concerned for humanity such helpful perceptions and images of the way to wholeness in our time.

Donald Grayston

Burnaby, British Columbia/
Cambridge, Massachusetts

Die natale TM
31 January 1984

THE DEVELOPMENT

OF A

SPIRITUAL
THEOLOGIAN

CHAPTER 1

THOMAS MERTON'S SEEDS AND NEW SEEDS

On 10 December 1968, twenty-seven years to the day
from the date of his arrival as a postulant to monastic
life at the Trappist-Cistercian abbey of Gethsemani in
Kentucky, Thomas Merton died accidentally in Bangkok,
Thailand.[1] Since his death, twenty-one new books have
appeared under his name;[2] so also have some twenty vo-
lumes[3] and some two hundred articles on his life and
thought by scholars and others. In these studies he is
variously seen as spiritual writer, religious thinker,
social ethicist/cultural analyst, literary entrepreneur,
and dialogical/transformational figure on two spiritual
boundaries--that between Christianity's past and future,
and that between Christianity and other faiths and
ideologies.

Walter Capps, for example, in his Hope Against Hope:
Moltmann to Merton in One Theological Decade, has called
him "the West's most influential fashioner of contemporary
spirituality."[4] He regards it as likely that Merton,
through his Asian Journal, will play a theologically cata-
lytic role in relation to the present generation similar
to that played by Dietrich Bonhoeffer through his Letters
and Papers from Prison in relation to the generation which
followed World War II.

> Both works, neither of which was completed because
> of the tragic deaths of their authors, include sug-
> gestions and embrace insights which are not fully

elucidated. In both instances, a design for the future is sketched in, though always only tentatively and partially. And yet the designs are both so fascinating and compelling that one can be sure that large future attention will be given to their fuller disclosure. Whereas Bonhoeffer projected Christian consciousness in transition (the content of which was elucidated in impressive fashion in the theology of hope), Merton gives indication of the restructuring of Christian sensibilities via an encounter with the full force of Asian religious experience.[5]
Whether or not Capps' scenario is ever fully realized, it remains true that Merton's stature as a figure of the highest importance in the contemporary reshaping of Christian spirituality is already an impressive one, and increasingly so.

But the dimensions of his stature have not yet been fully and clearly discerned, not least because of the complex reality of his person. To those who knew him only superficially, or whose minds could not distinguish paradox from inconsistency, he was a puzzling person, a man of temperament self-contradictory to the point of scandal--in the opinion of those scandalized, at least.[6] One journal, in issuing a commemorative number on Merton, could only try to do him justice by celebrating him as Cistercian, man of letters, liberator and reconciler, spiritual writer, literary catalyst, man of les grandes amitiés, and, very humanly, a man who "made a difference" to those who encountered in him a friend of deep integrity, a whole person of singular quality.[7] A more recent study, in comparable fashion, dealt with his rich complexity by describing him in relation to the various persons or constitu-

encies which claimed his interest or loyalty. Thus to his
brothers in the monastic community he was simultaneously
a true brother ("Uncle Louie") and a "playboy monk"; to
social activists with whom he corresponded, a temporarily-
misplaced activist himself; to Catholic peacemakers, their
prince in exile; and even, to Baptist seminarians, a fine
candidate (under somewhat different--and highly unlikely--
conditions) for the Baptist ministry.[8] A still later study
concentrates on his monastic vocation, subdivides it, and
adds to this growing list of categories those of solitary,
man of prayer, contemplative, ecumenist, monk of renewal
and Zen master.[9]

To those who knew him well, however, this paradoxical
and multi-faceted person was neither schizoid nor dilet-
tante, but a whole, creative and integrated human being,
conscious of his own imperfections, highly traditional
yet strongly unconventional.[10] Henri Nouwen, for one, asserts that Merton must be seen as "one of the most important spiritual writers of our century."[11] The late Thérèse
Lentfoehr, fellow-poet and his correspondent of longest
standing (from 1939 until his death), extends the time-
frame of estimation back to the founding days of Merton's
order.

> Since the days of St Bernard and the Golden Age of
> Cistercian mysticism there has not been a spokesman
> for contemplative life such as Thomas Merton. For men
> of all faiths he has been a pervasive influence ....[12]

And Benedictine historian of monasticism Jean Leclercq, in
his assessment, takes in the rest of the Christian centuries
in a statement which, if made by one less knowledgeable,
might be considered excessive: "I am not giving in to an
ingenuous, admiring expression of friendship when I rank

Merton with the Fathers of the Early Church and those of the Middle Ages."[13]

These assessments by personal friends are supported and nuanced by the judgements of scholars in the years since his death. Elena Malits, for example, one of the most perceptive students of his writings, quotes David Tracy as having remarked that Merton "may well turn out to be the most significant Christian figure in twentieth-century America."[14] Again in reference to his own nation, Lawrence S. Cunningham calls him the "foremost American spiritual writer of his generation."[15] John F. Teahan makes this more specific when he describes Merton as the outstanding representative in American mystical litera-ture of the apophatic strand within the Christian contem-plative tradition, and indeed its major representative in recent western Christianity.[16] Clifford Stevens makes the boldest assessment of all (which nonetheless I have not seen contested in print) when he asserts that people "of the twenty-fifth and fiftieth centuries when they read the spiritual literature of the twentieth will judge the age by Merton."[17]

In another group of assessments, a number of scholars have stressed that Merton's importance is chiefly a para-digmatic one, rather than being based on any original, constructive or systematic theological achievement in the usual sense. Indeed, they discern in Merton both the lack of theological originality as well as any desire for it on his part.[18] As a paradigmatic figure, however, they find him to be a person of considerable originality and contemporary fascination. Michael Zeik calls him "a sign for us of what the Christian of the future will have to be";[19] Cunningham says that he is a model for our day of

the "theologian in the ancient patristic sense of the word:
one who could speak existentially of the experience of God";[20]
Michael Casey suggests that his life is a "parable" which
incarnates and proclaims the "primacy of the spiritual" in
an apparently unspiritual age;[21] and Elena Malits, finally,
presents him as a "symbol and synthesis of contemporary Catholicism."[22] As with any true symbol, according to Malits,
Merton's hold on us is to be located in the power whereby
"it reveals us to ourselves, articulates what we may sense
but cannot say, and leads us into a future with new possibilities."[23] In aphoristic vein, she concludes that Merton
"not only employs metaphors, he is one."[24] I would want to
qualify her description of Merton as symbol and metaphor
by suggesting that he fulfills this role for contemporary
western Christianity as a whole, and not simply for the
Roman Catholic section of it, much less the American Roman
Catholic section, although admittedly, with each of these
constrictions, the symbolic connection becomes denser and
more intimate.

It is true, understandably, that Merton never put himself forward as a paradigm, becoming as the years passed
increasingly conscious of himself as a sinner, as one
who was still "on the way" or "on the edge": he was "ada-
mant, in fact, that he be taken neither as a paradigm of
virtue nor as a pattern of vocation."[25] For example, after
a discussion in his late and world-oriented journal, Conjectures of a Guilty Bystander, of Paul Evdokimov's view
of the monastic vocation as something outside history, on
the basis of which monks are better regarded as subjects
for "iconography, rather than character study," Merton
disagrees, and comments: "We are in history, for better
or for worse. We are not ikons .... We are men of prayer
and love, and being men of love we can move in the world

though unseen by it."[26] Then with his characteristic habit
of ending a serious discussion with a self-deprecatory
quip, he refers to the visit of the Red Cross "blood wagon":
"I ... discovered that I was in better health than last
year, weighing a hundred and eighty-five pounds, which is
certainly too much. As an ikon, I am not doing too well."[27]

However, it is not as a paradigm of _virtue_ that he
interests us, but rather as a paradigm of ascetical _process_
whereby the contemplative-out-of-the-world becomes the contemplative-at-the-heart-of-the-world.[28] Now that he is dead,
and we are able, in a preliminary way, to look at his life
all of a piece, we are strongly drawn, _pace_ his protests,
to consider the paradigmatic or ikonic aspects of his person.[29] In this regard, the phrase which in my view does
most justice to his many-sided witness and achievement is
ikon _of_ _Christian_ _wholeness_.[30] I find this term more satis-
factory than the others because it is both more suggestive
and more specific. As a biblical term, the word ikon di-
rects us to Christ the _eikon_ of God (cf. Colossians 1.15).
In Christian liturgy, it refers us to a sacred image
through which the reality of God and the church triumphant
can be experienced (cf. Cunningham's reference to Merton
as a theologian who speaks out of his experience of God).
In Merton's own Cistercian tradition, the restoration of
the likeness of the image of God in which human beings
are created is the goal of the contemplative life.[31] By
the modifier, "of Christian wholeness," I mean to refer
to his extraordinary capacity to give spiritual attention
to subjects as disparate as the Desert Fathers, nuclear
war, Shaker furniture and Zen meditation, his personal
openness to women and men of all faiths and none, and his
profound personal maturity and breadth of understanding.[32]

Thus it is for all these reasons that I see the truth of
Zeik's description of him as a sign to us, an image of
the Christian of the future: one who while remaining firmly
rooted in his own Christian tradition[33] reaches out to
other traditions and integrates their insights and wisdom
into his own. Taken together, terms such as "sign," "model," "parable," "metaphor," and "ikon" point us strongly
in the direction of what Sallie McFague TeSelle and others
have called "parabolic" or "intermediary" theology; and
this approach we shall explore in the next chapter as we
attempt to outline a biographical and autobiographical
hermeneutic for the texts we shall be examining.

This initial emphasis on Merton's person has been
a necessary one; for scholars are agreed that the assessment of his theological or ascetical accomplishment is
inseparable from continued reference to his person. Here,
for example, are three such assessments, made by an Anglican, a Baptist and a Roman Catholic, respectively. According to Robert Giannini, Merton by his entire life
has shown to activist Christians in particular

> a way in which they can be honest to their own se-
> cular selves while at the same time recognizing and
> honoring the mystical self that keeps making itself
> felt in the midst of busy and active lives.[34]

Glenn Hinson points us to the synthetic character of his
mind as a key to his achievement.

> When he fed through his resilient mind the teach-
> ing of the contemplative tradition with his an-
> tennae turned toward the modern world, a brilliant
> new product came forth .... In a remarkable way
> Merton put together the whole essential corpus of
> the Church's teaching on prayer. The one element
> which he added as the bond of it all was himself.[35]

And Jean Leclercq highlights his disposition to be a gene-
ralist rather than a specialist.

> The fact that he was not a specialist in anything
> (which would otherwise have limited his audience
> to other specialists) ensures the outreach of his
> message even to this day.[36]

It is still premature, I recognize, to form a fully
coherent or systematic account of his achievement as a
whole, either for this century or for Christian spirituality in general.[37] Nonetheless, beginnings can be made
and are being made in specific areas. I see this study
as one such beginning, examining as it will a self-limiting portion of the Merton corpus for what it can yield
concerning the evolution of one of his major works, and
concerning as well the direction and characteristics of
his development as a spiritual theologian writing in the
middle years of this century.

*

One useful way in which Merton's active intellect
and complex sensibility may be observed and understood
is by an examination of his manner of writing, which
was characterized by frequent and thorough-going revision.[38] Probably the prime example of this is the extensive and long-term revision of the work first pub-
lished as <u>Seeds</u> <u>of</u> <u>Contemplation</u> (Norfolk, CT: New Directions, 1949--hereafter <u>Seeds</u> or SC). This process
extended from at least 1948, and possibly earlier, to
1961, a period critical both for Merton's own journey
in the Spirit and for his theology. It was the period
during which he was passing over from his stance as a

theologically conventional member of a conservative order
in a conservative church to that of "universal man" or
transcultural believer.[39]

He completed the writing of Seeds, his first major
work of spirituality (his autobiography aside[40]), on 1
July 1948.[41] Then in his seventh year as a monk of Gethsemani, he was in his third year of monastic profession.
The book was published on 2 March 1949,[42] in the same
month in which he was ordained deacon. His ordination to
the priesthood, two months later, was followed (in his
thirty-fifth and thirty-sixth years) by eighteen months
of physical sickness and psychological upheaval.[43] From
this time of sickness he emerged as the substantially
whole person that his subsequent writings and the testimony of his friends and the students of his works reveal
him to be. He had dealt successfully, in large part, with
the problems he had taken with him into the monastery,
and in the course of his growth in contemplative life had
reached le point vierge.[44] From that point of personal
centering and integration he moved on and out to a deep
concern for social integration and the unity and spiritual health of the human race.[45] After his return to
health, he held teaching positions in the community for
fourteen years (1951-65), years to which we owe the
journals, much of the poetry, some lesser works of spirituality, and the articles on Zen, eremitism and peace
which grew into the books of the hermitage period (1965-
68). This last period was a very rich time for Merton,
a time when he was able more than ever before to follow
the solitary way to which he had been so strongly drawn
virtually from the time of his entry into Gethsemani.[46]

It was during the time of sickness mentioned above
that Merton produced the revised edition of Seeds (Nor-

folk, CT: New Directions, 1949--hereafter Seeds Revised or
SCR). He did this at a time when, as he notes in one
place,[47] he was almost incapable of writing, by which we
may take him to mean the creation of new works, rather
than the essentially editorial task of revising the already extant Seeds. Then early in the sixties, he published the much more thorough-going revision and amplification which is New Seeds of Contemplation (New York: New
Directions, 1962--hereafter New Seeds or NSC). Accordingly, there exist three published versions of what is or-
ganically one work.

At an earlier stage of this study,[48] I presented
a theological interpretation of the textual variation to
be found in these three versions by means of a close textual study of the lesser alterations and additions. Subsequently, a visit to the Thomas Merton Studies Center
at Bellarmine College in Louisville adverted me to the
existence of the original typescript of Seeds (hereafter,
TS1), and to the existence of the original typescript
(hereafter, TS2) of the major additions and amplifications
in New Seeds. Both TSS were then in the possession of Sr
Thérèse Lentfoehr, and are now, by her bequest, in the
collection of the Thomas Merton Center for Religious
Studies at Columbia University in New York. The catalogue
of her collection which she had prepared for the Center
at Bellarmine also contained a tantalizing reference to
a version of the text even earlier than TS1, in holograph, which a number of enquiries and the assistance of
many associates of Merton have failed to unearth.[49] However, through the kindness of Sr Thérèse in entrusting
the two TSS to me for an extended period, I was able to
collate them, together with the three published versions,

into an editio variorum (published simultaneously with
this study, also by The Edwin Mellen Press, as Thomas
Merton's Rewriting: The Five Versions of Seeds/New Seeds
of Contemplation as a Key to the Development of his
Thought). This variorum stands on its own as the definitive textual correlation to date of the versions of Seeds/
New Seeds considered as one work. As such, it is now a-
vailable to other scholars for whatever use they may wish
to make of it. In terms of this book it functions as
the foundation document for a theological study of Merton's development as a spiritual theologian over a dozen
or so years, critical ones for his growth as a man of the
Spirit. Readers of this study will find the variorum
useful but not essential; anyone wishing to challenge
any of my statements of fact or inference or wishing
to do a constructive theological or literary study of
Seeds and/or New Seeds will find it necessary to his or
her project.

By examining the changes he made in different passages as version succeeded version, we can observe Merton in the very process of his ongoing spiritual and
intellectual pilgrimage, something mentioned as a possibility by a number of critics, but only in passing.[50]
Methodologically, this is the strength of this study;
for by looking at five versions of one work by one author, in this case Merton, we can trace changes in tone
as well as in substance and area of interest with much
more precision than if we were looking at a number of
different works by the same author. The Waters of Siloe,
for example, was published in the same year as Seeds,
and The New Man in the same year (and month) as New
Seeds.[51] These pairs of books could probably be contrasted with each other, and the differences and deve-

lopments noted in a general way. But in the case of Seeds/
New Seeds, with perhaps fifty per cent or more of the text
of NSC having been carried all the way through from TS1,
the many editorial changes and additions become precisely
identifiable links to his theological and personal development. In sum, this study argues that by looking at the
variant readings within the variorum, we can trace and
document Merton's growth as a Christian contemplative and
spiritual theologian between the years 1948 and 1961.[52] I
suggest, in other words, that this study will enable us
to discern, by a textual method, the way in which Merton,
who in 1948 was essentially a world-denying and triumphalist monk, a contemplative-out-of-the-world, had by 1961
become a world-affirming and broadly ecumenical person,
a contemplative-at-the-heart-of-the-world, having in the
interim recovered Paradise, and having gone forth from
that recovery to the sophianic task of the building of
the Kingdom of God.

*

In this first chapter, I have outlined Merton's importance to contemporary Christian spirituality, and have
presented the argument that a theological study on the
textual basis of a variorum edition of Seeds/New Seeds
will enable us to trace and document the basic pattern
of his development during a critical period. In Chapter
2, I offer a brief outline of Merton's life. This is
hermeneutically important, inasmuch as many of the textual shifts in the variorum can be accounted for or correlated biographically. His birth, childhood and youth
(1915-41) is seen as bringing him, in his mid-twenties,

to a point of personal crisis at a time of world crisis.
The second and monastic half of his life (1941-68), spent
almost entirely at Gethsemani, is described in terms of
his own periodization, to which I have added a brief look
at the hermitage period. The chapter concludes with an
exploration of the usefulness of biographical or intermediary theology for a study of Merton's life and writings.
Chapter 3 sets out the theological character of TS1, the
first typescript. The text of TS1 is then linked at a
number of points to significant moments and themes in Merton's life, and is presented as an attempt on Merton's
part to record the inner side of the same spiritual journey the outer side of which he was describing in his autobiography and his journals. Chapter 4 discusses the beginning, in SC, of the work's refinement, both theological and literary. It situates SC within the tradition of
the encheiridion, or spiritual handbook, and suggests
contrasts with the examples of that tradition mentioned
by Merton. It goes on to examine passages from TS1 omitted in SC, passages rewritten, smaller emendations, passages missing from the text of TS1 as received, and passages entirely new in SC. Chapter 5 describes how in SCR
Merton makes a significant alteration in the tone of the
work, while leaving the essential framework of TS1 and
SC unaltered. The probable effects of Merton's respon-
siveness to his readers are noted; and TS1, SC and SCR
are considered together and characterized as a discrete
sub-group of texts.

With Chapter 6, we move on to the second sub-group
of texts, examining the larger developments, by means
of amplification or addition, which Merton made in TS2
to the text of SCR. TS2 is examined as the first docu-

ment in this second sub-group, and reasons and contexts for its emendations are sought. Chapter 7 presents NSC as the normative text, the final though still imperfect version of a modern spiritual classic, and the result of a long process of theological, spiritual and literary evolution. Chapter 8 tries to epitomize this final text within the context of Merton's mature spirituality by considering the notion of the recovery of Paradise as the fulcrum of his developed view of the contemplative life, with contemplation being seen on this understanding as a reality lived out in the service of the Kingdom, rather than as an end in itself.

The variorum (published separately, as I have mentioned above), set up in columnar form, contains the entire text of TS1, and all subtractions from, additions to or variations within this text made in the four later documents, together with two shorter related documents. References to the variorum in this study are made as follows: e.g., V 222--a reference to as many instances of the text in question as there are on that page; or, e.g., V 333, NSC--a reference to a particular version on a page. Other conventions used in the editing of the variorum are set out in the Prefatory Note to that work.

CHAPTER 2

MERTON: A BIOGRAPHICAL HERMENEUTIC

The name and person of Thomas Merton first became
familiar to large numbers of people with the publication
in 1948 of his autobiography, The Seven Storey Mountain.[1]
The book was for the most part written in 1944, at a time
when Merton was "still in the first flush of monastic euphoria and disgust with the secular world."[2] One critic
mocks it gently by calling it "that swan song of the
nineteenth-century monastic revival":[3] and it is true
that for most people reading it in the last quarter of
our century, its romantic and "gothick-monastick" passages stick out rather embarrassingly. But the same critic
is able to praise the book as well, for its intensely
moving and personal account of "a hunger and thirst, a
passion for God, which one rarely finds expressed nowa-
days."[4] Edward Rice, Merton's college contemporary and
godfather, in one of the less tendentious judgements in
his memoir of Merton, gives the following assessment of
its impact, locating its appeal in the skillful and moving way in which Merton evoked in it the flavor of what
it had been like to be young and without faith or hope
in those days.

> There are dozens of books with similar themes, yet
> this is the only one that touched a vital nerve in
> modern man. What makes it different from the others
> is its great evocation of a young man in an age
> when the soul of mankind had been laid open as never

before, during world depression and unrest and the
rise of both Communism and Fascism .... The war had
ended when the book appeared, yet Merton's apocalyp-
tic view of the world, of the suffering of Harlem
and the slums, his hatred of war, was even more valid. The Seven Storey Mountain was more than an odys-
sey into the Church. It was a confrontation of the
basic alienation of man with society, with the natural and supernatural forces that had nurtured him
over the centuries. But most of all it was a confrontation with Christianity, basically with Merton's
own vision of Catholicism. It was a great work, and
it touched almost everyone who read it.[5]

It was the book which created for Merton an immense reading public, and which thereby prepared the way for the
reception of his later books, including those which are
the subject of our present study. In Rice's comment may
be noted some of the matters with which these later works
would deal: the human being in his/her assaulted humanness, the human being in society, the possibility of
faith. Nor in reading this comment should we ignore, in
Rice's phrase, "Merton's own vision"--not simply of Catholicism, but of every subject on which he wrote. He
had a way, in writing, of opening himself personally
to his readers in a way that often precipitated an enormous response. "He excelled in making the reader feel
that he was close to him, that he even identified with
him."[6] This breadth and depth of appeal was signalled,
as far as the Mountain was concerned, by the fact (recorded by Rice and others) that it ultimately reached third
place on the non-fiction section of the American best-
seller list for its year of publication.[7]

The book opens with an archetypally Mertonian statement, a biblical/astrological/psychological (and melodramatic) view of his birth, at Prades, in the department of
Pyrénées-Orientales (mountains and the East! There is no
escape from the metaphors!) in southwestern France.

> On the last day of January 1915, under the sign of
> the Water Bearer,[8] in a year of a great war, and
> down in the shadow of some French mountains on the
> borders of Spain, I came into the world. Free by
> nature, in the image of God, I was nevertheless
> the prisoner of my own violence and my own selfish-
> ness, in the image of the world into which I was
> born. That world was the picture of Hell, full of
> men like myself, loving God and yet hating Him;
> born to love Him, living instead in fear and hope-
> less self-contradictory hungers.[9]

In more prosaic terms, he can be described as the elder
son of Owen Merton and Ruth Jenkins, artists then working in Europe, his father a New Zealander, his mother an
American. Soon after his birth, his parents fled the ha-
voc of contemporary Europe for the peace of Long Island,
the home of Ruth Merton's parents. There they settled
in the community of Flushing, where in 1918 Merton's
younger brother, John Paul, was born.

His father's religious background was Anglican, of
a certain degree of personal devotion, but with little
relationship to the community of faith; his mother's
was vaguely Protestant—she had also spent some time
with the Quakers.[10] Merton had been baptized at Prades,
apparently according to the rites of the Church of England;[11] but he was given no particular religious train-
ing or upbringing. In these early years, the occasion on
which his father's mother, then visiting from New Zea-

land, taught him the Lord's Prayer, stands out as a spiritual and catechetical high point.[12] His mother died in
1921, when he was six; and for the next four years he
accompanied his father on painting trips to such places
as Cape Cod and Bermuda, sometimes attending school and
sometimes not. It was what might now be called an unsettled childhood, and it was eventually to produce a tremendous appreciation on Merton's part for monastic sta-
bilitas. But at the time it seems to have been very much
to the liking of young Tom. "To me it seemed as natural
as the variations of the weather and the seasons. And one
thing I knew: for days on end I could run where I pleased,
and do whatever I liked, and life was very pleasant."[13]

By 1925 his father had made enough money from the
sale of paintings to return to France; and Tom, then
aged ten, went with him. They settled at St-Antonin, in
the Languedoc. As Merton describes them, the next four
years were a time of mixed experiences and feelings--
enjoyment of living in France and of being with his father, and loneliness when he was sent to board at the
Protestant lycée in nearby Montauban, to say nothing of
the turbulence of early adolescence.

In 1929 the Mertons moved again, this time to England, and Tom was sent to Oakham, an old public school
of something less than the first rank. Although as a
child the solitary conditions of much of his time had
already made him a great reader, it was during this period that he began to take a deep interest in serious
literature:[14] Blake,[15] Lawrence and Joyce were among his
favorites at that time. Only two years later, his father
died of a brain tumor, and Merton, aged sixteen, was left
in the care of his first godfather, a Harley Street spe-

cialist, who looked after his financial interests and arranged for his admission to Cambridge University, but does
not appear to have taken a very sympathetic interest in
him. After increasing disagreement between the two, and a
notable chapter of faults administered by his godfather
in regard to undisclosed misdemeanors,[16] Merton returned
to the United States in December 1934. As George Woodcock
notes,[17] it was a decisive moment for him: from that time
on he would live and work in the United States.

Again he lived with his mother's parents, and in
1935 entered Columbia, from which in 1938 he received a
BA. There his subjects ranged from law through geology
and philosophy to languages and literature. More important, however, both in his own view as in that of his bio-
graphers,[18] was the experience of taking part in the life
of a great university during a period of intense political
activity among the students, and the influence of the people he met there.[19] Among these Henri Nouwen marks out
as most influential four men.[20] These were Mark van Doren,
poet and professor of English, whom Merton credits with
having prepared his mind for what he saw in the mid-forties
as the "good seed of scholastic philosophy"[21] by the clarity and honesty of his teaching; Dan Walsh, professor
of philosophy, who first told Merton about the Trappists;
Bob Lax, Merton's closest friend at Columbia, who asto-
nished Merton in memorable fashion one day by telling him
that he should become a saint;[22] and Mahanambrata Bramachari, a young Hindu monk who moved in university circles,
and who told Merton about the Christian spiritual classics
at a moment when he was ready to listen.[23] Influential
also at this time, through his reading, were Etienne Gilson, whose Spirit of Mediaeval Philosophy showed Merton
that the notion of God was intellectually respectable

(chiefly by means of the concept of aseitas, God's own
being a se, in and from himself); Aldous Huxley, through
whose Ends and Means he discovered the mystical life; St
John of the Cross ("on the borders of Spain"), through
whose writings he began to encounter apophatic Christian
mysticism; and St Ignatius Loyola, with whose Spiritual
Exercises he seriously began the practice of mental prayer.[24] All these persons, contemporaries and long-dead
saints, men (all of them men) of three continents, were
thus involved in Merton's decision to enter the Roman
Catholic Church, into which he was conditionally baptized on 16 November 1938, at the age of 23.[25]

The next three years were pivotal ones. He finished
his MA at Columbia in 1939 (his thesis was "Nature and
Art in William Blake"), and then began to teach English,
first at the City College of New York and later at St
Bonaventure College (now University), near Olean, New
York. At the same time he was experiencing an increasing
desire to find a way to live out his baptism in terms of
a specific vocation. Thus in a letter of the period to
Ed Rice he describes his malaise of soul and his sense
of living an unfulfilled life.

> I am not physically tired, just filled with a deep,
> vague, undefined sense of spiritual distress, as if
> I had a deep wound[26] running inside me and it had
> to be stanched. ... The wound is only another aspect
> of the fact that we are exiles[27] on this earth. The
> sense of exile bleeds inside me like a hemorrhage.
> Always the same wound, whether a sense of sin or of
> holiness, or of one's own insufficiency ....[28]

As he would later theologize it, he was an exile from
Paradise, and the stanching of the wound of original sin

and alienation would require the recovery of Paradise through contemplation.

But in his first attempts to stanch the wound, he approached the Franciscans who ran St Bonaventure to discuss the possibility of entering their community. He was provisionally accepted, but later rejected on grounds which do not seem to have been made entirely clear to him at the time,[29] but which are commonly unstood to be related to Merton's frank disclosure of his wild-oats period preceding baptism. Then in Holy Week of 1941, at the suggestion of Dan Walsh, he visited the premier Trappist abbey of the United States: Gethsemani. Vocationally it was for him the decisive experience. Here he describes, in his journal of the time, the impact made on him by his first visit to his future home.

> This is the center of America. I had wondered what was holding the country together, what has been keeping the universe from cracking in pieces and falling apart. It is places like this monastery. ... This is the only real city in America. ... It is an axle around which the whole country blindly turns and knows nothing about it.[30]

Beneath and behind and through the hyperbole, the message is clear: he has found the the hospital where his wound can be stanched. His own personal universe, on the point of cracking in pieces and falling apart on more than one occasion, had now been re-connected to its archetypal axle or center. Privately he had for some time already been living as a religious, saying the breviary office and doing the Ignatian exercises. But this visit crystallized his intuition of vocation; and after a brief spell in Harlem with Baroness Catherine

de Hueck Doherty designed to test this intuition, he arrived at Gethsemani on 10 December 1941,[31] three days
after Pearl Harbor, to enter life-in-community among
the Cistercians of the Strict Observance.

Gethsemani was his home[32] for the next twenty-seven
years, the entire second half of his life. Until his final
trip to Asia, he seldom left it, apart from a few trips to
Louisville for medical reasons, some visits to other monasteries and convents,[33] and the notable trip on 22 June 1951
(also to Louisville) when he became an American citizen.[34]
Within the Benedictine/Cistercian perspective of stabili-
tas, or commitment for life to the monastery of one's profession unless moved by the community authorities, Gethsemani became the permanent home which as a child he had never had. It had been the lack of a real home which (especially after his father's death) had without question con-
tributed the greatest intensity to his search for the "one
good place,"[35] and thereby for personal wholeness.

Even so, it remains the judgement of his close asso-
ciate and sometime confessor and physician, John Eudes
Bamberger, now abbot of Genesee Abbey near Rochester, New
York, that "he never really felt completely at home or
accepted anywhere in his life."[36] The dislocation of his
early life and his disordered young adulthood had been
too damaging. Moreover, the power of his personality was
so intense that he could only find satisfying friendship
in an ever-deepening intimacy with God alone (cf. his
statement in New Seeds: "For there is only one thing that
can satisfy love and reward it, and that is You alone"--
V 78, NSC). Still, as Bamberger elsewhere specifies,
there is no doubt that it was Gethsemani that was the
place of his definitive spiritual and intellectual forma-

tion, the place of his recognizing and working through
all the crises of identity with which his gifts confronted
him.

> The Abbey of Gethsemani was the place where he achie-
> ved his identity as a man, a monk, a priest, a man
> of God, a poet and a prophet. For he was all of these,
> and he grew into them and developed in them in this
> one place.[37]

Merton himself says much the same thing when he states
that it was Gethsemani that

> taught me how to live. And now I owe everyone else
> in the world a share in that life. My first duty is
> to start, for the first time, to live as a member
> of a human race which is no more (and no less) ridi-
> culous than I am myself.[38]

*

Although we have followed Merton closely through the
critical events of his first twenty-seven years, we shall
not trace his second twenty-seven in like detail. Rather,
let us take note of Merton's own periodization of his
Gethsemani years, and then focus on the one specific time
within those years--the period of sickness already mentioned (see p. 9, above)--as the period of his life which
saw the beginning of his return to spiritual (as well as
literal) citizenship in the world which in 1941 he believed himself to have left forever. He established this
periodization[39] in his preface to A Thomas Merton Reader,
first published in 1962. At that time he distinguished
four periods:

> (1) 1941-44: his novitiate--a time of prayer, manual
>   labor, and initiation into monastic life;

(2) 1944-49: a time of assigned reading, writing and
translation, including his profession as a monk
and ending with his ordination to the priesthood;

(3) 1949-55: the critical time of sickness, followed
from 1951 by his work as Master of Scholastics
(students preparing for ordination); and

(4) 1955-62: his work of teaching and individual
spiritual direction as Master of Novices--which
continued until the end of this fourth period
in 1965 (but in which he was still engaged at
the time he outlined these periods);

to all of which we may now add

(5) 1965-68: the final years--the time in the hermitage and the journey to Asia.

Within this whole stretch of time, the period of sickness
which began what Merton identifies as the third period of
his life at Gethsemani stands out, in my view, as crucially important. To the student of Merton's life it appears as a separate period on its own. But it is at the
same time easy to understand why Merton, although describing it frankly in his journal, would not want to isolate
it from its consequences in his ongoing life in the abbey.
It was a bout of tremendous strain and upheaval which
seems to me to have been precipitated by two factors a-
bove all. The first of these was occasioned when Merton
reached the last of the institutional goals prescribed
for him by his membership of a Cistercian community of
the forties, namely ordination to the priesthood, which
at the time he called "the one great secret for which I
had been born."[40] The second, already mentioned, was
the writing and publication of his autobiography, which
seems to have effected in him a profound kenosis, a deep

self-emptying. This statement from The Sign of Jonas
gives his own account of what was happening to him in
this critical period.

> When the summer of my ordination ended, I found my-
> self face to face with a mystery that was beginning
> to manifest itself in the depths of my soul and to
> move me with terror. Do not ask me what it was. I
> might apologize for it and call it "suffering." The
> word is not adequate because it suggests physical
> pain. That is not at all what I mean. It is true
> that something had begun to affect my health; but
> whatever happened to my health was only, it seems
> to me, an effect of this unthinkable thing that had
> developed in the depths of my being. And again: I
> have no way of explaining what it was.

(Then, with the Mertonian freedom from consistency[41] which
any careful reader of his works soon comes to recognize,
he immediately sets about explaining it.)

> It was a sort of slow, submarine earthquake which
> produced strange commotions on the visible, psycho-
> logical surface of my life. I was summoned to battle
> with joy and with fear, knowing in every case that
> the sense of battle was misleading, that my apparent
> antagonist was only an illusion, and that the whole
> commotion was simply the effect of something that
> had already erupted, without my knowing it, in
> the hidden volcano.[42]

This was a mountain with fire in it, a fire which was
consuming the unfinished emotional business which Merton
had accumulated in his psyche. Nouwen sees this time of
spiritual darkness, which was also a time of physical de-
bility, as both "a period of terrible anxiety and uncer-
tainty"[43] and also as a "purification which prepared him

for a new task,"[44] teaching and caring for the students
and, later, the novices. What happened, says Nouwen, bor-
rowing the motif which Merton used for the title of the
journal in which he records these experiences, was that
"God called Jonas to go to the people, but Jonas fled to
solitude until God let him be brought back ... to where
his real calling lay."[45]

For at the deepest point of spiritual desolation
and loneliness in the monastic life which in a dramatic
act of fuga mundi Merton had embraced, he discovered his
fellow human beings: and his response, he found, could
only be one of compassion.

> It is in deep solitude that I find the gentleness
> with which I can truly love my brothers. The more
> solitary I am, the more affection I have for them.
> It is pure affection, and filled with reverence for
> the solitude of others. Solitude and silence teach
> me to love my brothers for what they are, not for
> what they say.[46]

As Sr Thérèse comments, "in discovering his inner solitude
he ... simply discovered what it is to be a man."[47] This
discovery unfolded in Merton because as monachos, as one
truly called to solitude, as one who realized in depth
the existential loneliness of the human being, he came
to know very deeply that he had

> entered into a solitude that is really shared by
> everyone. Even though he may be physically alone,
> the solitary remains united to others and lives in
> profound solidarity with them. ... He realizes that
> he is one with them in the peril and anguish of
> their common solitude: not the solitude of the indi-
> vidual only, but the radical and essential solitude
> of man ....[48]

"Yet," as Merton reflects in the same journal, "there is a return from solitude."[49] This return, <u>contemplata</u> <u>aliis</u> <u>tradere</u>, he accomplished chiefly through his writing, which he now began to understand as a means of giving away the fruits of solitude and contemplation. Merton expresses this thought by saying that to write something and to publish it was for him "to let go of my idea of myself";[50] and he also speaks of losing himself entirely "by becoming public property just as Jesus is public property in the Mass."[51]

So sickness had taken him into solitude, and solitude had returned him to health. For, as he says,

> in the depth of this abysmal testing and disintegration of my spirit, in December 1950, I suddenly discovered completely new moral resources, a spring of new life, a peace and a happiness that I had never known before and which subsisted in the face of nameless, interior terror. ... as time went on, the peace grew and the terror vanished. It was the peace that was real, and the terror that was an illusion.[52]

He had experienced that "pattern of disintegration, existential moratorium and reintegration on a higher level" which in one of his last (and most seminal) essays he was to say "is precisely what the monastic life is meant to provide."[53] As he emerged from the healing solitude, he found himself travelling in a different direction, that of a renewal of interest in and concern for the world which earlier he believed himself to have forever rejected. This new direction gradually changed his romantic view of the monastery as Paradise, or, otherwise stated, of Gethsemani as the place which could completely and permanently satisfy his longings for "home." New-born in spiritual autonomy, his own person became the prime vehi-

cle of his relation with and ministry to a most diverse
assemblage of visitors, correspondents, students, novices,
readers and colleagues.[54]   Two statements from his later
journal, Conjectures, can well be read together as comple-
ments providing in an ecumenical and inter-religious context a whole view of his mature understanding of his unitive vocation on behalf of the Kingdom of God.

> If I affirm myself as a Catholic merely by denying
> all that is Muslim, Jewish, Protestant, Hindu, Bud-
> dhist, etc., in the end I will find that there is
> not much left for me to affirm as a Catholic: and
> certainly no breath of the Spirit with which to
> affirm it.[55]

> If I can unite in myself the thought and the devo-
> tion of Eastern and Western Christendom, the Greek
> and the Latin fathers, the Russians with the Spanish
> mystics, I can prepare in myself the reunion of
> divided Christians. ... We must contain all divided
> worlds in ourselves and transcend them in Christ.[56]

These are statements from Merton at his most paradigmatic,
at his most ikonic. Because we know that Merton did unite
in himself the entire range of Christian spirituality
beyond even what he mentions here, we recognize in him
a paradigm for our own discipleship on the edge of the
third millennium anno Domini Jesu Christi. Because he
set for himself, or, better, accepted from God, the vocation to become--as a Christian--a whole human being, he
became an ikon of Christian wholeness for anyone who can
recognize him as he was. This is not a moral or hagio-
logical assessment, nor does it infer of Merton anything
that might be called perfection. It is, rather, an ascetical and cultural assessment, a sketching-out of how

Merton is perceived, how he functions at this point in
the ascetical journey of the Christian community.

*

We have traced thus far the path by which Merton came
to Gethsemani, and we have then focussed on his time of
existential sickness there. We have seen how he moved from
radical insecurity, through the compassion which he discovered and experienced in solitary contemplation, to a
life in which the opposites within his person (as Bamberger epitomizes them, his drive towards sociability and his
drive towards solitude[57]) could be related in a complementary and creative way, enabling him to hold together "the
living and fruitful contradictions and paradoxes of which
true life is full."[58] It simply remains now to record
that Merton's final journey had been undertaken in the
first instance in response to an invitation from Jean Leclercq to address a conference of leaders of Roman Catholic monastic communities in Asia, scheduled for December
1968, in Bangkok.[59] Having accepted this invitation, Merton then arranged an itinerary on which he could visit
a number of American and Asian monasteries and religious
centers, and could meet a number of religious leaders of
many faiths, notably the Dalai Lama.[60] And so it was in
Asia, many thousands of miles from Gethsemani, yet still
in a monastic setting, and thereby still "at home," that
Thomas Merton died.[61]

*

This emphasis on Merton's person as the prime vehicle of his ikonic vocation leads us directly to the re-

cently-developed genre of theological exploration which
goes under such names as "parabolic" or "intermediary"
theology. For the purposes of this genre, biography and
autobiography have been seen in recent years by a number
of theologians as sources for a theology which is immediate, concrete and sacramental. Autobiography, for example,
or as Harvey Cox calls it, "testimony," gives to the reader

> the first-person account of the teller's struggle
> with the gods and demons. It begins inside the
> speaker and says, "This is what happened to me."
> Recently neglected, testimony deserves reinstate-
> ment as a primary mode of religious discourse. It
> is a genre which celebrates the unique, the ec-
> centric and the concrete. ... It reclaims personal
> uniqueness in an era of interchangeability.[62]

Autobiographical theology, a sub-species of intermediary
theology, is neither parable nor systematics, but a theology which attempts to contribute to the systematic
task by keeping close to the parabolic elements within
Christian literature.[63] It is a theology which "attempts
to serve the hearing of God's word for our time by keeping language, belief and life together in solution."[64]
By its concrete rendering of events and circumstances,
spiritual autobiography points to the mystery of the
self in relation to God--which is of course the precise
concern of ascetical or spiritual theology. This concrete
rendering enables the autobiographer's fellow-disciple
to read his or her account of his or her life for ascetical reasons: to find out about one's own life, to compare one's own coming-to-faith with that of another,
and to correlate one's own story and the author's with

the normative story for Christians, the story of Jesus.
It is really then the reader who makes it possible for
autobiography to be read as theology, to become a source
of theological reflection, by perceiving and then sharing the perception that one's reading of it has served
the hearing of the word of God in one's own time and
place.

More concretely than other genres, intermediary
theology seems to many to be able to provide immediacy
and authenticity in an age when abstract and highly-
conceptualized kinds of theology seem less and less
able to touch, to carry meaning, to inspire. Lonergan
is awesomely systematic, but he reaches few immediately:
which is not to say that as his work is mediated by
others to the faith-community over the years he will
not affect the way we think about our faith. By reflecting, however, as James McClendon suggests, on "singular
or striking lives, the lives of persons who embody the
convictions of the community ... but with new scope or
power,"[65] we are provided with hermeneutical tools for
reflecting on our own lives. A useful way to apply
this hermeneutic is to find dominant or controlling i-
mages in the lives and thinking of the particular persons who interest us theologically. By "images" here,
McClendon means

> metaphors whose content has been enriched by a
> previous prototypical employment so that their
> application causes the object to which they are
> applied to be seen in multiply-reflected light;
> they are traditional or canonical metaphors, and
> as such they bear the content of faith itself.[66]

He cites as examples the ways in which Dag Hammarskjöld
refined the image of servant, and in which Martin Luther

King reshaped the images of exodus and Promised Land for
their contemporaries.[67] By reshaping a canonical metaphor
in a way inseparable from their persons, these men became
"vivifiers"[68] of their religious traditions. Through their
reminting of traditional and biblical images for their
faith-communities, they laid powerful claims for attention and respect on those communities.

That Thomas Merton was another such person there
can be little doubt. According to Elena Malits, whose
articles on Merton have so far concentrated on this area,
Merton throughout his adult life was engaged in the telling of his story.

> Augustine had done it, and Thomas Merton returned
> us to autobiography as a form of theological dis-
> course. It appears to me that such is Merton's
> real significance as a spiritual writer.[69]

He had, she believes, a highly-developed facility for
articulating his experience "as a person undergoing
transformation in an anguished era of history and in
the life of the Church,"[70] a facility exercised through
autobiography in such a way that other persons living
in the same anguished era found it striking and in-
sight-bearing.

If then following McClendon we look for the "controlling image" in Merton's life and writings, we need
look no farther than contemplation. As Bamberger affirms, "The one word ... that best sums up Merton's
spiritual teaching is contemplation."[71] By the form of
his life, with its catholic interests, even more than
by his writings, he reminted the concept of contemplation, or, to put it more personally, that of the contemplative. By this I mean that he embodied and con-

tinues to embody the contemplative potentiality of his
"community"--variously the abbey of Gethsemani, the
Cistercian order, the Roman Catholic Church, the entire
Christian community, even the human race--in which he
takes his place as the "holy man of our time"[72]--but in
a new way, and in his own unique way. He took a traditional or canonical metaphor, contemplation, and gave
it new scope and power as a contemporary category.[73]

He did this partly, even mainly, through his explicitly autobiographical works--the Mountain and the
journals. But as Malits points out, almost all of his
writing

> might be described as having an autobiographical
> dimension. In his articles on Zen, social issues,
> contemplation, or what have you, he was engaged
> in communicating his own consciousness of these
> realities and what difference they made in his
> life.[74]

Beyond the professedly or explicitly autobiographical
portion of his writings, therefore, she encourages us
to examine others of his works for their implicitly
autobiographical content. Merton himself can be cited
in support of the viability of this approach in regard
to the first published version of the work under consideration in this study, Seeds of Contemplation. When
he received a copy from his publisher, it provoked
the following reaction, not in this case a very happy
one: "Every book that comes out under my name is a
new problem. ... Every book I write is a mirror of my
own character and conscience."[75] Accordingly, when we
take Merton at his word, we are stimulated to read Seeds
and New Seeds in the context of his developing contemplative life. By placing them in sequence, and by reading

them through the filters of his autobiography and the two
journals of the same period, we will be able to trace
something of his spiritual and theological development,
something of his reminting of the image of the contemplative in the Church from the time before his critical
sickness to the time of high productivity and maturity
in the early sixties. For our reading of TS1, SC and SCR
(1948-49), the Mountain and The Sign of Jonas (which covers the period from December 1946 until July 1952) will
be our chief companions. For our reading of TS2 and NSC
(1961), Conjectures of a Guilty Bystander (which contains
material recorded between 1956 and 1965) will serve a
similar function. By attempting to correlate the implicitly autobiographical testimony of Seeds and New Seeds
with some of the explicitly autobiographical testimony
of the Mountain and the journals, we will try to bring
together the two sides, inner and outer, of a single
journey.

   It is the journey of Thomas Merton, monk and poet,
on his way back from exile and wounding, and forward
on the high road of contemplation to the place of wholeness in the spirit, to the recovery of Paradise.

CHAPTER 3

TS1: <u>SEEDS</u> IN TYPESCRIPT

With an examination of TS1, we begin the documentary portion of this study, a portion which carries on through this chapter and Chapters 4-7. Each of these chapters follows the same outline: a brief bibliographical introduction; a theological characterization of the text in question, together with an integration at specific points of the inner and outer sides of Merton's journey; and a brief conclusion.

*

TS1, the earliest text <u>known</u> to exist, was for many years in the possession of Sr Thérèse Lentfoehr, of Racine, Wisconsin. During the many years when he had no secretarial assistance, Merton sent materials to Sr Thérèse to be typed; with his permission, she often kept the original manuscript or carbon copies of the typescript. Together with the rest of her collection of Merton materials, TS1 is now at the Merton Center at Columbia. Existing in one copy only, it consists of 126 sheets of typescript on manila paper eight-and-one-half inches by eleven inches, each typed on one side only, and bearing on many of the sheets emendations in Merton's crabbed and difficult handwriting. The folder containing it carries the notation "Seeds of Contemplation; Top Copy of First Draft," with

the words "Top Copy" suggesting the existence, at least
at one time, of one or more carbon copies.

The first three sheets, containing the front matter
for the published version, are unpaginated in the original. In the variorum they are designated as V [i-iii].
Pages 1-51 contain the prologue ("Seeds of Contemplation") and the text of Chapters 1-12. Pages 52-58 contain the first part of Ch. 13, with the second part of
Ch. 13 found on the three pages following: "a," "b," and
"c" (in the variorum, "58/a," "58/b," and "58/c"--V 261-
68, 271-73). This obvious break in Merton's overall pa-
gination, the fact that they are typed in a fainter
typescript, and the fact that the text on p. 59 is of
the same intensity as that on p. 58 mark these three
pages (which deal with the Virgin Mary) as a passage
written later than the main body of TS1.

Pages 59-89 correspond to Chs. 14-20 of SC; and pp.
90-93 and 95 (94 is missing) to the greater part of Ch.
21. Pages 96-103, the entire text of Ch. 22 of SC, are
also missing from TS1. Chapters 23 and 24, pp. 104-14,
are both found in the typescript, but Ch. 25, pp. 115-19,
is also missing.[1] The last two chapters of SC, 26 and 27,
are found on pp. 120-34. The last page of the typescript,
p. 134, bears the date of 1 July 1948, with the notation
added, "Vigil of Our Lady's Visitation," the date which
also appeared in SC when it was published in the following year.

The sheet which I have called TS1a (V 3-4) is a
Latin poem in the form and style of a mediaeval office
hymn. The text, in both original and improved versions,
is found on a MS of one page, also in the Lentfoehr collection. It is written in Merton's handwriting, and it

appeared, again with minor improvements, in SC, and for
the last time, in form identical with that in SC, in SCR.

*

In the prologue of TS1 (V 27-34), which bears the
same title as the book to be published some months later,
we find all the elements which we will need to bear in
mind as we read along: the "seeds" themselves, and the
soil in which they can spring up; the slavery of sin and
the freedom of life in Christ; and the love, will and
purpose of God for human lives. The "seeds" are those
"germs of spiritual vitality that come to rest impercep-
tibly in the minds and wills of men" (V 27), seeds that
will perish and be lost unless they fall into "the good
soil of liberty and desire" (V 27) prepared for them in
the hearts of human beings. They are "seeds of freedom"
(V 29) which will be rejected by anyone whose mind is
still "the captive of its own natural desire" (V 29: in
SC, Merton drops the--for him--pejorative term "natural").
Yet, accepted by those whose hearts are prepared, they
will "spring up one day in a tremendous harvest" (V 30)
of glory to God and joy to humankind.

The "seed" image is of course as old as Christianity, if not older. The parable of the sower (Matthew 13)
comes at once to mind: here the seed is the word of God.
In 1 John 3.9, the writer speaks of "God's seed" (<u>sperma
theou</u>) remaining in the one who is "born of God." It was
an image of which some of the early Cistercians, notably
Aelred of Rievaulx, and George Fox and the early Friends,
made considerable use. Merton had used the image and
its development, "seeds of contemplation," in a short
work published in 1948, <u>What Is Contemplation</u>?

> The seeds of this perfect life [the life of contemp-
> lation] are planted in every Christian soul at Bap-
> tism. But seeds must grow and develop before you
> reap the harvest. There are thousands of Christians
> walking about the face of the earth bearing in their
> bodies the infinite God of Whom they know practically
> nothing.
>
> The seeds of contemplation and sanctity have
> been planted in those souls, but they merely lie
> dormant. They do not germinate. They do not grow.[2]

By contrast, it will be the "great anxiety" (V 33: in SC,
more soberly, the "chief care") of those who do love God
to receive and do his will, and thereby fulfill his purpose in their lives.

> And by receiving His will with joy and doing it with
> gladness I have His love in my heart because my will
> is now the same as His love and I am on the way to
> becoming what He is, Who is Love (V 33).

The run-on sentence is a good reflection of Merton's fer-
vency of spirit at this time, of the generosity of the
young monk who wishes to be whole-heartedly generous with
a generous God.

With a grasp on these elements, the reader is equip-
ped to read on in a lucid and engaging, if somewhat over-
heated, treatise on individual piety, one that offers a
severe call to contemplation, a generous dash of contemp-
tus mundi, and a thoroughly traditional Bernardine/ scho-
lastic/Carmelite diet of spirituality. However, the reader
will find little of social or even of domestic import,
little for "the world" but the contempt of an author who
is glad to have "escaped" it, and the strong implication
that the thoughtful, single and male reader who pursues

the author's argument to the end and agrees with it will
do well to make the appropriate response and join him
in his monastery. In fact, some 2000 postulants came to
Gethsemani in the forties and fifties, many, especially
after 1948, attracted by Merton's writings.[3]

Chapter 1 ("Everything that is, is holy") begins
the development of this argument. Yes, "the world and
everything made by God is good" (V 41, cf. 148): but the
problem is that

> until we love God perfectly His world is full of
> contradiction.[4] The things He has created attract
> us to Him and keep us away from Him. They draw us
> on and they stop us dead. We find Him in them to
> some extent and then we don't find Him in them
> at all (V 44).

Only when we belong, in a deeply realized sense, to God's
love, will we be able to "own all things in Him and offer
them all to Him in Christ His Son" (V 42). Tree, fish
and mountain give glory to God in accord with his purpose, by existing as they were intended to exist. No
two of them are exactly alike, but "their individuality
is no imperfection" (V 48: "individuality" is not a pejo-
rative term for Merton; "individualism" is).

> This leaf has its own texture and its own pattern
> of veins and its own holy shape .... the great,
> gashed, half-naked mountain is another of God's
> saints. There is no other like it .... and that is
> its sanctity (V 51).

In this focus on concreteness and individuality, Merton
may be seen foreshadowing Cox and TeSelle and other intermediary theologians in their emphasis on the ikonic
power of the particular. The mountain, however, achieves
the "inscape" (V 50--G. M. Hopkins' term) which is its

sanctity without conscious effort; but human beings find
themselves in a very different situation. We are captives
in the "prison of our own self-hood" (V 43, cf. 29, 30).

> To say I was born in sin is to say I came into the
> world with a false self. I came into existence under
> a sign of contradiction, being someone that I was
> never intended to be and therefore a denial of what
> I am supposed to be. And thus I came into existence
> and non-existence at the same time ... (V 56).

This statement takes us directly back to the opening paragraph of The Seven Storey Mountain; and with the image of
the prisoner of contradiction, the implicitly autobiographical element of the text has surfaced.

> Free by nature, in the image of God, I was neverthe-
> less the prisoner of my own violence and my own self-
> ishness, in the image of the world into which I was
> born.[5]

This being so, "the problem of sanctity and salvation is
in fact the problem of finding out who I am and of discovering my true self" (V 52-53); for the "false self" is
only an "illusory person," a "private self ... who wants
to exist outside the radius of God's will and God's love"
(V 57). "True self" and "false self" are not further e-
laborated in TS1; but the reader familiar with the New
Testament scriptures will find them easy to correlate
with the concepts of flesh and spirit (cf. Romans 7.25,
Galatians 5.16-17).

> Merton, as he begins the search for this "true self,"
finds that he must attempt to solve the

> one problem on which all my existence, my peace and
> my salvation depend: to discover myself in disco-
> vering God. If I find Him, I will find myself and

if I find my true self I will find Him (V 60).
He recognizes that the only one who can teach him to
find God, and thereby his true self, "is God, Himself,
Alone" (V 61); and he recognizes also that, "like a word
seeking to discover the Voice Who utters me," he will
never actually make this spiritual discovery "if I look
for that voice outside myself" (V 61). In his own spiritual center, however, "at the point where I spring out
of nothingness and am held in being by His love for me"
(V 62), he encounters God, who begins to live in him
"not only as my Creator but as my other and true self"
(V 68: emphasis Merton's).[6] In baptism, Merton asserts,
the false self has died "a true and formal death" (V 69)
in the soul of the believer. However, since "natural activity tends in one way or another to bring back to life
the false self," the "problem of finding God and finding
myself in Him is not solved by Baptism alone" (V 69).

Here again Merton is referring to his own experience. His baptism into the Roman Catholic Church at the
age of 23 had been a profound experience for him, as he
tells us in his autobiography.

As November began, my mind was taken up with this
one thought: of getting baptized .... I was about
to set foot on the shore at the foot of the high,
seven-circled mountain of a Purgatory steeper and
more arduous than I was able to imagine, and I was
not at all aware of the climbing I was about to
have to do.

The essential thing was to begin the climb.
Baptism was that beginning, and a most generous one,
on the part of God. ... But my human nature, my
weakness, and the cast of my evil habits still remained to be fought and overcome.[7]

He was later of the opinion that he should have embarked
immediately after his baptism on a program of spiritual
direction and daily communion.[8] So when he speaks of falling back "into the confusion of ambitions and pleasures
and anxieties that blind me and corrupt me" (V 70), he
is basically recalling how "he made such a mess of that
first year after my Baptism."[9] Eventually, as we know,
he made a definite decision about what would be necessary for him if he was to maintain his Christian life
with any degree of fervor.

> To seek God perfectly means this: to withdraw from
> illusion and pleasure and worldly anxieties and
> desires; to keep my mind free from confusion in
> order that my liberty may be always at the dispo-
> sal of His will ... (V 78).

He offers this statement to the reader in the abstract;
but for himself, in the perspective of his post-baptismal
slackness, we recognize that it refers to his decision
to "withdraw" from the secular world, and to become a
monk at Gethsemani.

> Having done so, he found himself faced then with the
temptation, common to those of his state, to believe that
he was holier than others. Again the reference is indi-
rect.

> There are still some who erect themselves pedestals
> of knowledge or virtue or apparent sanctity and
> climb on to them in order to breathe a different
> atmosphere from other men and above all to enjoy
> the difference for its own sake, thanking God for
> their distinction from the rest (V 84).

This temptation (or fear) is easily understandable as
part of the effect of his having left 20th-century New

York for (so to speak) 17th-century France: for Trappist
life in the forties in the United States had changed very
little from the time of Abbot de Rancé and the renewal
of Cistercian life at La Trappe. The memorable passage
where he breaks definitively with this illusion is one
of the loci classici of his spiritual experience.

> In Louisville, at the corner of Fourth and Walnut,
> in the center of the shopping district, I was sud-
> denly overwhelmed with the realization that I loved
> all those people, that they were mine and I theirs
> .... It was like waking from a dream of separateness,
> of spurious self-isolation in a special world, the
> world of renunciation and supposed holiness.
>
> ....
>
> This sense of liberation from an illusory dif-
> ference was such a relief and such a joy to me that
> I almost laughed out loud. And I suppose my happi-
> ness could have taken form in the words: "Thank God,
> thank God that I am like other men, that I am only
> a man among others." To think that for sixteen or
> seventeen years I have been taking seriously this
> pure illusion that is implicit in so much of our
> monastic thinking.
>
> ....
>
> I have the immense joy of being man, a member
> of a race in which God Himself became incarnate. ...
> if only everybody could realize this! But it cannot
> be explained. There is no way of telling people that
> they are all walking around shining like the sun.[10]

Yet having recognized that he will not be able to find
himself "by isolating myself from the rest of mankind
as if I were a different kind of being" (V 87), he still
has to struggle with the authentic dimensions of solitude.

He can only justify solitude in the monastic sense by the
"conviction that it will help you love other men better"
(V 88). "Go into the desert not to escape other men," he
simultaneously admonishes the reader and himself, "but
in order to find them in God" (V 90). Only in the intersubjective unity in which love of God, neighbor and self
coinhere will he reach the goal of the spiritual search;
and no evasion is possible for the sincere searcher if
this reality is to be attained. "For Love is my true identity. Selflessness is my true self. Love is my true character. Love is my name" (V 101-02: this last surely in
the Old Testament sense of "name," as somehow conveying
to those who know the name the reality of the person to
whom it refers).

In Merton's presentation of it, the mystical life
is frequently one of paradox: and one of the greatest paradoxes consists in the contemplative's realization that
he cannot pass through the center of his own soul into
God unless he is able to "give himself to other people
in the purity of selfless love" (V 106: emphasis Merton's),
a process made possible, even in solitude, by the bond
among believers in the mystical body of Christ.

> ... when I enter into my own deepest self I find
> you by passing through myself into Christ, Who is
> you and Who you are, and Who I am: and so in the
> depths of contemplation I will find you, myself
> and Him (V 109, cf. 113, 114).

That so few take this view and adopt the contemplative
way has resulted in the "body" of the human race becoming
a "body of broken bones" (V 119). This is particularly
evident in the division among believers within the Christian community, and by the way in which unceasing divisive-

ness among human beings generally widens out into war,
even the possibility of the "cosmic inhumanity of atomic
war" (V 122). So it is that those who adopt the way of
love must expect to experience pain, "some suffering by
our very contact with one another because this love is
the resetting" (V 123) of the broken bones in God's body
among human beings. Once again, this must be accomplished
in a solitude in which we can grow "in love for God and
in love for other men" (V 134); and in one of the few
references immediately applicable to the non-monastic
reader, he advises the finding of a particular room or
corner which can be used undisturbed for prayer on a re-
gular basis (V 136-37).[11]

Later in this same chapter, Merton delivers himself
of a series of ascetical admonitions which taken together
perhaps constitute the low point of the book, in terms
of purported objectivity, at least. As spiritual direction to anyone living in the world, they are, taken at
face value, ludicrous. But as a summary of warnings to
himself about the different aspects of what he considered
his dissipated former life, they are at least understandable.

> Do everything you can to avoid the amusements and
> the noise and the business of men. Keep as far away
> as you can from the places where they gather to
> cheat and insult one another, to exploit one ano-
> ther, to laugh at one another, or to mock one ano-
> ther with their false gestures of friendship. Do
> not read their newspapers, if you can help it. Be
> glad if you can keep beyond the reach of their
> radios. Do not bother with their unearthly songs
> or their intolerable concerns for the way their
> bodies look and feel and smell.

Do not smoke their cigarettes or drink the
things they drink or share their preoccupation with
different kinds of food. Do not complicate your life
by looking at the pictures of their women in magazines (V 139-41).

On almost every point in this passage he modified his
opinion in the later versions. But behind the revulsion
which permeates this passage lies a continuing sense of
his own weakness, and his conviction that only in monastic
life would someone as weak as he be able to find salvation.
Related to this is his somewhat romantic preference for
rural life over urban,[12] and his suspicion of the city
as the place of moral destruction: Harvey Cox describes
him as the "poetic prosecutor of the city."[13]

Breathe God's air. Work, if you can, under His sky.
But if you have to live in a city and work among
machines and ride in the subways and eat in a place
where the radio makes you deaf with spurious news
... do not be upset but accept it ... as a seed of
solitude planted in your soul ... (V 143-44).

A later passage, ten further paragraphs in this vein
(V 145-46), is omitted in SC.

Another passage of high revulsion, crossed out by
Merton in the text of TS1 itself, is this summary comment
on life at the lycee, on the chaplain at Oakham, and on
the rector of Zion Episcopal Church, Douglaston.[14] "The
principal effect of five centuries of protestantism (sic)
has been to make all religion seem like well-meaning
stupidity" (V 154, cf. 200). It would have been fairer
to say that up to this point he himself had not encountered any representatives of Protestantism that he could
respect intellectually. In this regard, his description

of "Buggy" Jerwood, the unfortunate chaplain at Oakham,
is as devastating as it is memorable.

> ... his religious teaching consisted mostly in more
> or less vague ethical remarks, an obscure mixture
> of ideals of English gentlemanliness and his favorite
> notions of personal hygiene.
>
> ....
>
> His greatest sermon was on the thirteenth chap-
> ter of First Corinthians .... But his exegesis was
> a bit strange. However, it was typical of him and,
> in a way, of his whole church. "Buggy's" interpre-
> tation of the word "charity" in this passage ... was
> that it simply stood for "all that we mean when we
> call a chap a 'gentleman.'"
>
> ....
>
> I will not accuse him of finishing this chapter with
> "Now there remain, faith, hope and gentlemanliness,
> and the greatest of these is gentlemanliness ..."
> although it was the logical term of his reasoning.[15]

A later comment in a long section (V 199-201) omitted in
SC refers to the conclusion about the meaning of life to
which the modern world has come "after having been taught,
for five centuries, a concept of faith which is nothing
but an evasion" (V 200). The link-phrase, "five centuries," would seem to lay this disaster as well at the
guilty door of Protestantism, although 500 years would
take us back to the fifteenth century, which may mean
that the Renaissance is being tarred with the same brush
as the Reformation. Later, his reading of Barth and Bonhoeffer, among others, would bring him into touch with
Protestant theologians whom he found eminently worthy
of his respectful interest.[16]

Once again, this time in Ch. 8, we find him turning

his sharp pen against himself, with a description of the deluded expectations with which people enter monastic life.

> Perfection is not something you can acquire like
> a hat--by walking into a place and trying on several
> and walking out again ten minutes later with one
> on your head that fits. Yet people enter monasteries
> with that sort of idea.
>
>   They are very eager to get the first available
> system fitted on to them and spend the rest of their
> lives walking around with the thing on their heads
> (V 164-65).

In Merton's own case, this meant complete initial devotion, in the name of monastic obedience, to the scholastic theology then dominant throughout the Roman Catholic Church, a theology for which he believed his exposure to the lectures of Mark van Doren and Dan Walsh had providentially prepared him.[17] Later, as we shall see, he was to conclude that biblical, patristic and intuitive approaches to theology were better suited to contemplative life than the rational and philosophical approaches of his early years in the monastery.[18]

   Then towards the end of Ch. 9 occurs (V 177) a passage ("At the root of all war is fear ...") which proved to be the seed of the most notable contribution, in NSC, to his social spirituality.[19] In TS1, however, it is more an illustration, in social terms, of an atomistic piety, than it is a genuine contribution to a social one. The fear which is at the root of war is the fear of everything, which is generated by the inability of human beings to trust themselves or others; and they "cannot trust anything because they have ceased to believe in God" (V 178). Only a restoration of love for and trust in God will

enable them to "love the men they cannot trust" and to
"dare to make peace with them, not trusting in them but
in God" (V 184). Combined with this must be a renunciation of any hate for the makers of war. Rather, says
Merton, "hate the appetites and the disorder in your
own soul, that are the cause of war" (V 190). The commen-
dation of satyagraha and non-violent social action as
elements in a fully social spirituality is a very long
way off. But in the meantime, Merton's abhorrence of
war, born of his antipathy to the strife-torn world of
the late thirties,[20] is registered here for the later
development it will receive in the late fifties and
early sixties.[21]

Throughout the book, the sense of the immense reality of the living God is one of the givens. Very different had been his experience at Oakham, where in the
course of religious instruction he had been exposed to
Descartes' proof of his own and God's existence, and had
for a time accepted it. Later, however, he rejected it
on experiential grounds of two kinds: the experience of
being a member of a church directed by a magisterium,
and the experience of God in darkness which his temperament found more directly convincing than any attempt to
reach God through conceptualization. Here he recounts
his introduction to Descartes, at Oakham.

> I accepted the Cogito ergo sum with less reserve
> than I should have, although I might have had
> enough sense to realize that any proof of what is
> self-evident must necessarily be illusory. ...
> If Descartes thought it was necessary to prove his
> own existence, by the fact that he was thinking,
> and that his thought therefore existed in some
> subject, how did he prove that he was thinking in

the first place? But as to the second step, that God
must exist because Descartes had a clear idea of Him--
that never convinced me, then or at any other time,
or now either. There are much better proofs for the
existence of God than that one.[22]

Rather, says Merton, now maturing as a contemplative,

... the Living God, the God Who is God and not a
philosopher's abstraction, lies infinitely beyond
the reach of anything our human intellects can grasp
as evidence. Or, if you prefer it, His immensity is
so close to us that it overwhelms us altogether.

And therefore He Who is infinite Light is so
immense that our minds see Him only as darkness (V
203).

Because no human word or concept can adequately express
this "immensity" ("incomprehensibility" might in this context have been a better term) of God, the contemplative
must pass beyond all that can be seen or heard into the
darkness and silence, the obscurity and emptiness in
which alone the "God Who is God" can be found (cf. V 204).[23]
In this darkness, God infuses the light of contemplation
into the mind and heart of the contemplative, but in a
way which bypasses the senses which are incapable of
receiving or conveying his full reality; and since "it
does not pass through the eye or the imagination or
reason, this light, this certitude is ours without any
vesture of a created appearance, without any likeness that
can be visualized" (V 206). In this experience, the contemplative's capacity for intuitive openness is much more
important than his capacity for rationalization of the
experience--even though this is attempted in just such
a work as we are considering. So, says Merton, "It is a

naked and simple and immediate intuition. You either get
it or you don't" (V 206; omitted in SC).

Similarly, the simplest way for a person with
thoughts of a contemplative vocation to proceed, in Merton's view, is to submit himself to the authority of the
teaching Church, rather than to attempt to reason his
way into a contemplative state.

> If you believe, if you make the simple act of sub-
> mission to the authority of God proposing some
> article of faith externally through His Church, you
> will receive this interior light which is so simple
> that it baffles description and so pure that it al-
> most seems coarse to call it an experience (V 207-08).

Merton's account of Father Moore's sermon at Corpus Christi
in New York records his own first experience of what this
kind of submission could involve. The sermon

> was not long: but to me it was very interesting to
> hear this young man quietly telling the people in
> language that was plain, yet tinged with scholastic
> terminology, about a point in Catholic Doctrine.
> How clear and solid the doctrine was: for behind
> those words you felt the full force not only of
> Scripture but of centuries of a unified and continu-
> ous and consistent tradition. And above all, it was
> a vital tradition: there was nothing studied or
> antique about it.[24]

This was in the summer of 1938, some few months before
his baptism. His discovery of the Roman Catholic Church
as the bearer into modern times, and by implication into
the future, of a "unified and continuous and consistent
tradition" made a deep and lasting impression on him,
something directly related to his own sense of rootless-
ness and to the pre-war tension through which he and mil-

lions of others were suffering at the time. The transcendent Church would, he felt, offer him stability in a
world gone mad; and its divinely authoritative teaching,

> revealed to us in the Scriptures and confirmed by
> the ... powerful unanimity of Catholic Tradition
> from the First Apostles, from the first Popes and
> the early Fathers, on down through the Doctors of
> the Church and the great scholastics, to our own
> day[25]

would liberate him from the necessity of creating on his
own a viable understanding of God and the universe, an
enterprise in which he felt himself up to that point to
have been totally unsuccessful. His excessive use of
capital letters in the passage just quoted bears witness
to the power of the impact on him of his first encounter
with ecclesia docens, both in terms of admiration and
relief.

But as a man of the twentieth century, a man "living
on the doorsill of the Apocalypse, a man with veins full
of poison, living in death,"[26] it was the vitality of
the Catholic tradition, more than its antiquity, which
commended it to him. In TS1, he develops this early impression by describing the Church as, paradoxically, "at
the same time essentially traditional and essentially
revolutionary" (V 217). The tradition of Christianity,
however, "supernatural in its source," must not be con-
fused with "human traditionalism" which can only tend to
"stagnation and lifelessness and decay" (V 218). It accom-
plishes its divine task, and hence may truly be called
revolutionary, by continuing in each succeeding genera-
tion--and normally in judgement on each generation--to assert the unchanging truths of Christian revelation.

> This is the most complete revolution that has ever
> been preached: in fact it is the only true revolu-
> tion, because all the others demand the extermina-
> tion of somebody else, but this one means the death
> of the man who, for all practical purposes, you have
> come to think of as your own self (V 222).

Here speaks "Frank Swift," failed Communist, who has discovered that what is needed is a personal revolution
rather than a social one, although he is eager to point
out the changes in society which would come about if enough
such individual revolutions took place.[27] By accepting
Catholic dogma, Merton has delivered himself/been delivered
from his previous "system" (hardly the right word) that
was "vague and fluid, a system in which truths pass like
mists and waver and vary like shadows" (V 227). Only an
unshakeable dogmatic foundation can give him the security
he requires to pursue his quest: and such, according to
Merton, has been the testimony of all the great saints, who

> arrived at the deepest and most vital and also the
> most individual and personal knowledge of God pre-
> cisely because of the Church's teaching authority,
> precisely through the tradition that is guarded and
> fostered by that authority (V 228).

Here personal and corporate knowledge of God meet and con-
join; the contemplative's personal faith is at one with
the faith of his community, and he is released from the
pursuit of speculation to follow his intuitions of God
in the darkness of contemplation.

After sections on the humanity of Christ in contemplative prayer (V 235-49), on the Eucharist (V 255-58),[28]
and on the Blessed Virgin Mary (V 262-68, 271-73), all
of them quite conventional in their piety, if a little
baroque in their expression, we come to a brief and inte-

resting discussion of the hermit vocation in Ch. 16, "Freedom under obedience." Merton begins the chapter with some basic affirmations about the growth of fraternal charity through the cenobitic life of obedience and forbearance. Virtually any other cenobite of the period could have ended the chapter without a consideration of eremitism. But as we know from The Sign of Jonas, Merton was already struggling with his drive towards greater solitude. He speaks there of finding, in deep solitude, "the gentleness with which I can truly love my brothers,"[29] of entering the desert of solitude and finding that its true name and nature is compassion.[30] Paradoxically, his discovery of compassion in solitude was the result of his work as Master of the Students.

> I do not know if they have discovered anything new, or if they are able to love God more, or if I have helped them in any way to find themselves, which is to say: to lose themselves. But I know what I have discovered: that the kind of work I once feared because I thought it would interfere with "solitude" is, in fact, the only true path to solitude.[31]

He had proved by experience a truth that he had earlier intuited, that the desert of solitude is "not necessarily a geographical one";[32] and that he could live in union with Christ, "the hermit who is the center of history,"[33] at the same time as he was ministering to the scholastics and was continuing his work of writing. So he speaks in January 1950 of having effectively renounced his "dream of a hermitage";[34] and in April of the same year he calls this dream, which had evidently returned to him in the interim, "reprehensible."[35] His "Carthusian" temptations had subsided over the same period;[36] he concluded that

the reason why God had permitted him to experience them
was so that he could counsel those in the scholasticate
who had the same problem.[37]

But while he was writing TS1, the struggle for solitude was a very active one, and struggle in concrete, geographical terms: he wanted at least to have a hermitage
on the abbey grounds. Something of his inner dialogue
of the period comes through in this passage from TS1.

> There is always a danger that hermits will only
> dry up and solidify in their own eccentricity.
> Living out of touch with other people they tend to
> lose that deep sense of spiritual realities which
> only pure love can give.
>
> Do you think the way to sanctity is to lock
> yourself up completely with your prayers and your
> books and the meditations that please and interest
> your mind and protect yourself with many walls a-
> gainst the irruption (<u>sic</u>) of people you consider
> stupid? ... Do you imagine you will find God by
> winding yourself up in a little cocoon of stuffy
> intellectual pleasures instead of renouncing all
> your tastes and desires and ambitions and satisfac-
> tions for the love of Christ Who will not even live
> within you if you cannot find Him in other men?
> (V 302-03)

There is no direct answer in TS1 to these rather irri-
table questions. But the answer was to come through his
experience as monastic teacher and writer, in which he
was to taste the truth of his own belief (stated in a
passage immediately following the preceding quotation),
that "interior contemplation and external activity are
two aspects of the same love of God" (V 303).

Closely related to this theme is his treatment of

monastic obedience: his abbot had in fact required him to
promise that he would not continue to try to become a Carthusian before he would authorize his ordination as a sub-
deacon.[38] His references to the relation of the contemplative and the abbot (V 307-09) are clear indications that
Merton is writing subjectively. By his acceptance of a superior as a "mediator between him and God" (V 308) he had
found a bulwark against the conflicting desires which continued to plague him even after seven years in the monastery. Another passage dramatizes how he saw his own tendency to self-will in this connection.

> ... the most dangerous man in the world is the con-
> templative who is guided by nobody. He trusts his
> own visions. He obeys the attractions of an interior
> voice but will not listen to other men. ... And if
> the sheer force of his own self-confidence communi-
> cates itself to other people and gives them the im-
> pression that he is really a saint, such a man can
> wreck a whole city or a religious order or even a
> nation: and the world is covered with scars that
> have been left in its flesh by visionaries like
> these (V 309-10).

This is an alarming passage. There is a kind of negative
inflation at work which suggests that Merton's struggle
with the strength of his own ego is near breaking point.
Few readers would have given any credence to Merton's
suggestion that a disobedient or self-inflated contemplative could wreck a nation, of course:[39] what was ar-
guably true of Bernard of Clairvaux and the twelfth century was manifestly not true of a cloistered writer in
Kentucky in the twentieth. The real significance of this
passage lies in the witness it gives to the struggle in

the soul of an apparently self-confident man one of whose
closest friends, Bob Lax, had once made a deep impression
on him by telling him that he should not be content to be
less than a saint.[40] Another remark from the period of
this struggle gives a more realistic expression of how this
was to be accomplished.

> If I am to be a saint--and there is nothing else that
> I can think of desiring to be--it seems that I must
> get there by writing books in a Trappist monastery.
> If I am to be a saint, I have not only to be a monk
> ... but I must also put down on paper what I have
> become.
>
> ....
>
> One of the results of all this could well be a com-
> plete and holy transparency: living, praying and
> writing in the light of the Holy Spirit, losing
> myself entirely .... Perhaps it is this, after all,
> that is to be my way into solitude.[41]

And so it proved, for the major period of Merton's time
at Gethsemani. When authorization for him to be a hermit
finally came in 1965, he had worked through these con-
flicts of monastic identity to which TS1 testifies, had
found his place in the world at the monastery, and had
begun to share the fruits of contemplation with many
others, a sharing which was not simply an overflow or
an act of supererogation, but an integral part of his
vocation.[42]

The tension between contemplation, narrowly conceived, and external activity, conceived more in terms
of the life he had left behind than in monastic terms,
had now reached a critical point of synthesis. As long
as he saw them as inimical realities, his presentation
of contemplation could appeal only to very few persons,

the circumstances of whose lives involved them very little
in "external" activities. But by integrating the two no-
tions, even in the very limited way indicated in the passages quoted about solitude, Merton had begun a process
which would later be clearly seen as open-ended. He was
refashioning his own understanding of contemplation for
a world of action.

TS1 provides further evidence that for Merton, "contemplation" had become nothing less than a metaphor for
the totality of the Christian life, at least as he was
then living it himself.

> Contemplation ... is the reason for our creation by
> God. ... All those who reach the end for which they
> were created will therefore be contemplatives in
> heaven: but many are also destined to enter this
> supernatural element and breathe this new atmos-
> phere while they are still on earth (V 365-66).

To say that contemplation is the reason for the creation
of human beings is to make a very bold and unusual claim;
but Merton is able to make a case for it in a way which
links up with the more usual apologetic for our creation.
Through contemplation, he says, both in the experience
itself and in the orientation it provides for a person's
life, God draws us "utterly out of our own selfhood"
and into his own "immensity of liberty and joy" (V 370).
The soul, in contemplation, is restored to "something
like the situation of Adam and Eve in Paradise" (V 373),
that is, to the condition of the union with God and
with each other which God intended, in the creation, for
all humankind. A mature contemplative will not feel torn
between his union with God and his union with his neighbor. That thought, according to Merton, falsifies any

authentic discussion of what contemplation really is by
positing an adversary relationship where none exists.[43]

> In practice what sanctity, what experience of God,
> what love of God, what purity of soul can divide
> love against itself and separate the love of God
> in Himself from the love of Him in men? ... God
> does not give His joy to us for ourselves alone,
> and if we could possess Him for ourselves alone
> we would not possess Him at all. Any joy that
> does not overflow from our souls and help other
> men to rejoice in God does not come to us from
> God (V 442-43).

Even so, this does not mean that the sharing of contemplation will be easy. There may be some apparent dissipa-
tion of the gift of contemplation in an attempt to share
it: in sharing it the contemplative may "leave a stain
on the pure emptiness where God's light shone" (V 443),
or at least may feel that "it is intolerable for him to
speak about it as his own experience" (V 444: emphasis
mine). In this last phrase we have a revealing indication of the nature of the text. It is in many ways, as
we have seen, something written out of Merton's own experience of contemplative life. But because to make it
explicitly autobiographical would be to invite something
close to "physical pain" (V 444), he chooses to focus
on a general and theoretical presentation of contemplation, and to downplay his own experience--which nonetheless keeps showing through.

The last chapter ("Pure Love") begins by summarizing
"three degrees" (V 456--in SCR, "three modes") of contemplation. The first, a "clean breath of understanding"
which comes relatively rarely, is a "sudden emptying
of the soul in which images vanish and words are silent"

(V 456). The other two modes can be habitual states. One
of these is the experience of aridity, of interior suffering, in which to rest is to experience the assurance
of God's presence even in darkness and dryness. The o-
ther is the experience of "the cloud," of a "tranquillity
full of savor and rest and unction" (V 457), a communion
in obscurity with the divine Christ. They are three possible "beginnings" (V 460) of the inner experience of
contemplation--hence Merton's alteration of "degrees" in
TS1 to "modes" in SCR (cf. V 473); and each one of them
may be a threshhold to a step that is "not a step" (V
469).

> When the next step comes, you do not take this step,
> you do not know the transition, you do not fall into
> anything. You do not go anywhere, and so you do not
> know the way by which you got there or the way by
> which you come back afterwards. ... What happens is
> that the separate entity that was you suddenly dis-
> appears and nothing is left but a pure freedom in-
> distinguishable from infinite Freedom, love identi-
> fied with Love (V 468-69).

In this intersubjective relation, it is of course the
false self that has vanished, with the true self being
united with God. This is not entirely clear from the passage above, which states that "the separate entity that
was you suddenly disappears," with no elaboration in
terms of false or true self. In SCR, Merton altered
this to "the separate entity that is you apparently disappears" (V 469). Thus in the fullness of contemplation,
made possible by the gradual eradication of the false
self in the approach to contemplation in one or other
(or, more than one) of the three modes described, even

the true self is united to God in an experience which at
the time is not distinguishable from absorption. In other
words, contemplation is not experience at the time of its
being experienced; but, as Merton comments, it "becomes
an experience in a man's memory" (V 470), that is, in his
own memory.

And even this is, in its turn, only a beginning (V
473); it remains for the contemplative to desire fully
and uninterruptedly that God's will be done for God's
own sake, and to desire God to be God in totality and
eternity. Thus

> it is in these two desires perfectly conceived and
> fulfilled that we are emptied into Him and trans-
> formed into His joy and it is in these that we
> cannot sin. ... Therefore it is something that all
> who desire to please God ought to desire--not for
> a minute, nor for half an hour, but forever (V 478-79).

Merton's description of the experience of contemplation,
as we have summarized it, is of course a traditional
one, in terms of doctrine or concept. But in this same
chapter occur passages, such as the following one, which
mask their autobiographical origin only by the thinnest
overlay.

> Suppose such a man were once in his life to vanish
> into God for the space of a minute.[44]
>
> All the rest of his life has been spent in
> sins and virtues, in good and evil, in labor and
> struggle, in sickness and health, in gifts, in sor-
> rows, in achieving and regretting, in planning and
> hope, in love and fear. ... In all these things his
> life has been a welter of uncertainties. ... But
> in the moment of time ... in which he was delivered
> into God ... there is no question that then his life

was pure; that then he gave glory to God; that then
he did not sin; that in such moment he could not
sin (V 477-78: cf. Augustine's non posse peccare).
The rest of the chapter reunites the contemplative vocation he has found, and which in the passage above he
has all but proclaimed as his own, to that of his brothers
in the contemplative community. Recalling again that his
claims for contemplative life must be considered in the
light of his use of the term "contemplation" as a metaphor for the totality of the Christian life, we are presented with a conclusion to TS1 incandescent in its intensity, and we are invited to share, if we will, in that
incandescence.

It is in these souls that peace is established in
the world.

They are the strength of the world, because
they are the tabernacles of God in the world. They
are the ones who keep the universe from being destroyed.[45] They are the little ones. They do not
know themselves. The whole earth depends on them.
... They shall inherit the land. ... They alone
appreciate the world and the things that are in
it. They are the only ones capable of understanding
joy. ... They are the clean of heart. They see God.
He does their will, because His will is their own.
... They reach out for us to comprehend our misery
and drown it in the tremendous expansion of their
own innocence, that washes the world with its
light.

Come, let us go into the body of that light.
Let us live in the cleanliness of that song. Let
us throw off the pieces of the world like clothing

and enter naked into wisdom. For this is what all
hearts pray for in the cry: Thy will be done"
(V 479-81).

Thinking of the published version, Anthony Padovano sees
in our text the hand of the poet, in a way reminiscent
of Dante, particularly in the last two chapters. "There
is," he says, "a purity about them, a suffusion of light,
a contemplative sensitivity, a profound, poetic, moving
quality."[46] I certainly grant this: and yet it also seems
that it was the very poetry of the work, when it came to
be published, which salvaged the emotional harshness and
the theological extremism which mars both the original
text and SC. Four further rewritings would be needed to
bring poetry, thought and feeling to the maturity of
<u>New</u> <u>Seeds</u>.

                              *

   TS1 is the work of a passionate and articulate contemplative, writing in the most orthodox fashion of the
apophatic tradition. Yet if it is read <u>only</u> as an objective account of the contemplative experience of Catholic
Christians, a major part of its significance is missed
and its fascination underestimated. If, however, it is
read as an integration, however partial, however inchoate,
of Merton's own experience in our historic time as a contemplative within that tradition, then it can be seen in
its true light. It is in fact a summary statement of the
inner side of Merton's own spiritual journey, the outer
side of which we can read in <u>The</u> <u>Seven</u> <u>Storey</u> <u>Mountain</u>
and <u>The</u> <u>Sign</u> <u>of</u> <u>Jonas</u>.

CHAPTER 4

SC: THE FIRST PUBLISHED VERSION

Seeds of Contemplation was published by New Directions, then of Norfolk, Connecticut, and now of New York,
best known as publishers of contemporary poetry (including some of Merton's), on 2 March 1949.[1] It comprised
one blank leaf, with the front matter on pp. [2-12], the
text itself on pp. 13-201, and two blank leaves at the
end. Measuring 22 by 14.5 cm, it was handsomely bound
in a tan burlap cloth, moving one of its reviewers to
remark that it was "garbed like a monk."[2] Merton, when
he received his copy March 5, recorded the comment of
his publisher, James Laughlin, that "the burlap effect
on the binding is a material they are using now in
night clubs for wall covering"[3]--perhaps a way of
saying to himself (and to others, when the comment was
published) that in his role as a writer he had not
really left the world behind, and also, perhaps, a way
of suggesting that the work was less valuable than its
readers might be inclined to think. A signed edition,
of 100 copies in brown slipcases, was issued the same
day as the first edition, something which caused Merton
misgiving.

> I find myself thinking about ... how to distribute
> signed complimentary copies of the de luxe edition
> of this book. I should never have gone into such
> a thing as a boxed special edition. I must be
> crazy.[4]

As the first major work[5] published by Merton after The
Seven Storey Mountain, it was warmly welcomed by the
large readership which the autobiography had attracted.

    It received eleven reviews (that I was able to find),
largely favorable.[6] Emile Cailliet, writing in the Journal of Religion, saw it as "evidently destined to become
a devotional classic," and recorded his feeling that whole
sections were autobiographical.[7] The anonymous reviewer
in the Times Literary Supplement called it "fresh, direct
and keenly felt."[8] Merton's own reaction, once he had
the book in his hands, was mixed. He begins euphorically--

    Yesterday Seeds of Contemplation arrived and it is
    handsome. I can hardly keep my hands off it.

but the euphoria is short-lived.

    Every book that comes out under my name is a new
    problem. To begin with, each one brings with it a
    searching examination of conscience. ... I always
    open the final, printed job, with a faint hope of
    finding myself agreeable, and I never do.

      There is nothing to be proud of in this one,
    either. It is clever and difficult to follow, not
    so much because I am deep as because I don't know
    how to punctuate .... It lacks warmth and human
    affection. ... I don't see how the book will ever
    do any good.

    . . . .

      The Passion and Precious Blood of Christ are
    too little in the book--only hinted at here and
    there. Therefore the book is cold and cerebral.
    What is the good of trying to teach people to love
    God without preaching through those wounds?[9]

This last comment is of special interest for his state-

ment of purpose in writing the book, so casually included:
"to teach people to love God." His other comments, at this
remove, seem hypersensitive and prickly, although the remark about punctuation is germane, if one objects to run-on
sentences and the over-use of piling-up nouns or adjectives
for effect. Following publication, excerpts were published
in two periodicals--The Catholic Worker, 15.12 (April 1949)
3, and the Liguorian, 38 (1949) 431. The text used in the
variorum is that of the fifth printing.

*

When Seeds was published, it was introduced and commended to its readers by an "Author's Note," (V 10-13)
not found in TS1. In this introductory statement, Merton
calls it "the kind of book that writes itself almost
automatically in a monastery," and "a volume of more or
less disconnected thoughts and ideas and aphorisms about
the interior life" (V 10). Both of these statements may
fairly be questioned. Admittedly, it was a book which
clearly issued from monastic experience; but the intensity and contemporaneity of the writing (if not the subject-matter), and the lived quality of its assertions
(evident to Merton's friends, such as Sr Thérèse, who
speaks of him as "unabashedly" writing about his closeness
to God, and of writing out of personal experience[10]) made
it a book which had not been and could not be written
"automatically" in any monastery other than Gethsemani,
nor by any person other than Thomas Merton. If it was the
kind of book Merton describes, one wonders why there was
not a glut of such "automatic" books on the market. Merton is also unfair to himself and the book when he calls

it "disconnected." Chapter 9 ("The Root of War is Fear"--
in NSC it has been renamed "Sentences": V 169-71, 176-78,
184-85, 188-90) comes the closest to this description.
But even if there is not an explicit or systematic structure to the book, there is observably a continuous forward movement, beginning with considerations of the human
condition in the context of creation, fall and redemption
(Chs. 1-5), continuing with an examination of aspects of
the contemplative journey in its early stages (Chs. 6-20),
and concluding with explorations of mature contemplative
experience (Chs. 21-27).

Later in the "Author's Note," Merton situates the
book in what he calls the "long tradition of such writing"
(V 11), that is, the tradition of the encheiridion, or
spiritual manual/handbook (although he does not use the
term). Again, the examples he cites are open to question,
both in terms of being good parallels for SC as well as
in terms of their place in the encheiridion tradition.
Pascal's Pensées is indeed disconnected and aphoristic,
lacking the basic structure we have identified in SC.
The Cautelas and Avisos of St John of the Cross[11] are
very much shorter, and nowhere near so comprehensive.
The Meditationes of Guigo, also much briefer, are much
narrower in their subject-matter. Only The Imitation of
Christ is a good parallel for SC in scope, substance
and intimate tone.[12] But having mentioned these works,
Merton immediately shrinks from the suggestion that he
is comparing his own writings with those of their au-
thors, and says that he is mentioning them simply "to
justify the publication of what is nothing more than
a collection of notes and personal reflections" (V 11)
such as might have occurred to any Cistercian--thoughts
which were "put down on paper when there was time, with-

out order and without any special sequence" (V 11).[13] He
admits, however, that he has then rearranged these notes
into the general order we have discerned, and expanded
them "where details seemed to be required" (V 11), an
indication that TS1 itself is a reworking of earlier material (probably recorded in the lost notebooks, since
no major rearrangement takes place in SC).

Continuing to qualify the nature and limits of the
book, he tells the reader that everything in the Gospel,
the Rule of St Benedict, and the Catholic ascetical tradition must be assumed as background; and within this
tradition he points to the 12th-century Cistercians and
St John of the Cross as his chief authorities. His stated
hope in having written SC is "that it does not contain
a line that is new to Catholic tradition or a single word
that would perplex an orthodox theologian" (V 12). Further
disclaimers follow: that the book is not a work of art
(a number of commentators refer to the charm and lumino-
sity of the writing--see above, p. 63, n. 46); and that
anyone else with the same interests could have written it
(impossible, as we have already seen, because of its intensely autobiographical texture). The note concludes with
an encouragement to the reader to read the book "in communion with the God in Whose Presence it was written,"
a statement which is immediately and rather nervously
balanced with the wry comment that "if you cannot read
it under these conditions, no doubt the book will be at
least a novelty" (V 13). The unsettled tone of this introductory Note supports Clifford Stevens' judgement that
the book was

> incomplete in its vision of man and immature in its
> judgement of "the world," but [that] its passion and

its pain made it the common voice of the seeker of
God, and the peace and tranquillity of its moods
brought something of the monastic quiet to the reader.[14]

It was a work with rough edges, and within the year Merton was to set to work on smoothing them down as he prepared the first published revision, SCR. This process of
development, however, was already well advanced in terms
of the modifications to TS1 which appear in SC. Here we
shall consider them under the following heads:

    (a) omitted passages;

    (b) rewritten passages of some length;

    (c) smaller emendations;

    (d) passages missing from the text of TS1 as received;
       and, finally,

    (e) three entirely new passages (i.e., in addition
       to the "Author's Note," also new in SC).

*

(a) <u>Omitted Passages</u>

In addition to omitting numerous words, phrases and
sentences throughout the work, Merton omitted from SC
seven major passages found in TS1. In the first instance,
from Ch. 3 ("Pray for your own Discovery"), he omitted
a passage of two paragraphs (V 74-75) dealing with the
nominal or perfunctory living of Christian faith, a passage which would seem, together with others in TS1, to
refer to his own post-baptismal slump (cf. V 70: see also
pp. 41-42, above). Probably he omitted it because the
concern of the passage is already covered in the preceding
section (V 73-74), and also, perhaps, because its omission
provides for a more direct transition between the passage

preceding and the passage following. With these two paragraphs gone, the reader goes directly from "Even though
my soul may be justified ..." (V 74) to the magnificent
prayer, "Justify my soul, O God ..." (V 75). The link is
formed by "justified/justify"; and in his prayer for justi-
fication, Merton prays that the sacramental sharing in
the righteousness of Christ which he received in his baptism may be made real in a victorious encounter with the
deadly sins which were marring his early life as a baptized adult. A similar concern for more direct transition and the desire to avoid repetition accounts for the
omission of a later passage on love for God and for others
in God (V 100-01).

Another omitted passage (mentioned above, p. 46),
deals with the solitary vocation from a perspective of
apatheia, or detachment, even as regards such basic matters of human life as dwelling-place, occupation and
companionship (V 145-46).

> Do not prefer one place to another: and you will
> learn to be alone wherever you are.
>
>   Do not prefer one occupation to another, and
> you will learn to be alone in everything that you
> have to do.
>
>   Do not prefer the company of one man to that
> of another, or the company of men to the company of
> none, or even being alone to being with others: then
> you will be alone when you are in the midst of men
> (V 146).

There is a Carthusian chill worthy of Guigo himself on
this passage, and this may have been why Merton decided
to omit it from SC. Certainly it was not because the chapter in which it occurs (Ch. 6, "Solitude) was already too

long, consisting as it does of only three printed pages.
It should also be recognized that the writing level in
this chapter is rather fine, an important consideration
for Merton. I can only conjecture (judging, for example,
by the excerpt that I have included) that Merton at this
point in his life, even in spite of the attraction to
solitude which was eventually to take him to the hermitage, found himself shrinking from the severity of his
own thoughts, and allowed his impulse towards gregarious-
ness to pull him back from so bleak a presentation of the
call to solitary life. From the point of view of Merton's
struggle to find balance in his monastic life, another
omission (V 163-64) parallels this last. It deals with
the way in which "artists and saints" (V 163) can be un-
nerved, even destroyed, by an opposition which causes
them to rely on their false selves, or else to retreat
from aggressivity into a passivity which passes for do-
cility. Such persons

> let other people absorb them into their own myth.[15]
> They allow any sort of abstraction to be imposed
> upon them and they never grow up and become real
> (V 164).

But the tendency to react to opposition with hostility is dealt with in the paragraph preceding, and the
temptation to passivity in the paragraphs immediately
following; and so the passage was omitted with no damage
to the continuity of thought. A further passage, this
one on the light of faith (V 208), Merton removed from
Ch. 11 ("Faith"). Having just stated that this interior
light "is so simple that it baffles description" (V 207),
he had then begun to describe it, at least in terms of
its effects. The omission of this attempt at description
thus allows the earlier statement more validity than

when it was, as in TS1, immediately ignored.

Finally, two passages are omitted which deal with
the acceptance of a monastic authority. The first (V 312-13)
contrasts the freedom which a monk gains from basing all
his activity on a principle above himself with the freedom
of worldly independence. The second contrasts the less
dangerous position of a person who finds himself or herself
constantly struggling with lust or temper with the more
dangerous position of one "who has complete control over
his carnal appetites and does not know how to renounce
his own judgement" (V 336). The themes of both are adequately
covered, as with the other omissions, by the context.

(b) Rewritten Passages

SC contains seven rewritten passages of some length.
Three of these concern faith (V 196-201, 207-08, 210-11).
The others are concerned with God's initiative in contemplation (V 61-67), pride (V 83-87), coinherence in the body
of Christ (V 105-18), and humility (V 160-63).

The first of these occurs in Ch. 3 ("Pray for Your
Own Discovery"), and concerns what Merton will later call
le point vierge. The shift in his treatment of this "meta-
phorical apex of existence" (V 61) lies in the direction
of greater emphasis on the initiative of God in the formation of contemplatives. In TS1 there is the implication
of a guarantee. There he refers to the point "at which I
will meet God by a real and experimental contact with His
infinite Being" (V 61). In SC, he describes it as a point
"at which I can meet God in a real and experimental contact
with his infinite actuality" (V 61, emphasis mine). This
pair of parallels suggests the general tone of the shift.

I am like a word seeking to discover the Voice Who
     utters me (V 61, TS1).

God utters me like a word containing a thought of
Himself (V 61, SC).

Contemplation is actively brought to birth in a human person by the God who "speaks His own name in the center of
your soul" (V 64), who "comes down from heaven and finds
us" (V 65). Merton's emphasis in TS1 was on the God who
is "present in everything as Creator" (V 66) and yet who
"cannot be grasped or known" (V 66) by his creatures, but
remains at a great distance from them, "not in the distance of space but in the far greater distance of natures
infinitely separate" (V 67). This is replaced in SC by an
emphasis on God's presence in all things "by His knowledge
and His love and His power and His care of them" (V 66).
This God is a God who "bridges the distances between Himself and the spirits created to love Him, by supernatural
missions of His own Life" (V 67). The presence of God in
creation and his presence through incarnational love are
found in both texts; but the emphasis is on the first in
TS1, rather abstractly, and on the second in SC.

A second rewritten passage occurs in Ch. 4 ("We Are
One Man"). In TS1, Merton had spoken of those who try to
raise themselves above others "with an imaginary holiness"
(V 83), who "erect themselves pedestals of knowledge or
virtue or apparent sanctity and climb on to them in order
to breathe a different atmosphere from other men" (V 84).
The effect of their lives is to make the very idea of
sanctity odious to those who have no personal idea of
what true holiness is. In SC, he names this disease. It
is spiritual pride, of a kind that "gets into the hearts
of the saints and eats their sanctity away before it is
mature" (V 83). In the paragraphs in SC which parallel
the text as found in TS1, there is a notable intensifica-
tion of the feeling of revulsion at such persons, but the

syntax remains in the plural. Then in the latter part of
the passage, developing out of it but without parallel
in TS1, it shifts to the singular.

When a proud man thinks he is humble his case is
hopeless.

Here is a man who has done many things that
were hard for his flesh to accept. He has come through
difficult trials ....

The pleasure that is in his heart when he does
difficult things ... tells him secretly: "I am a
saint." ...

The pleasure burns into a sweet devouring fire.
The warmth of that fire feels very much like the love
of God. ...

He thinks his own pride is the Holy Ghost.

The sweet warmth of pleasure becomes the cri-
terion of all his works. ... He is so pleased with
himself that he can no longer tolerate the advice
of another--or the commands of a superior. ...

After that he is ten times as stubborn as
before (V 84-87).

The singular form and the intensely personal tone mark
this as a passage in which Merton's experience of his
own growth in holiness, in conjunction with his incomplete self-acceptance, have produced a statement of intensely painful self-accusation, an undeniable je m'accuse
in spite of the use of the third person. As in TS1, this
passage is followed in SC by a discussion of the antidote
to the disease, the search for God in others (V 87-88,
90). The Louisville experience, which took place sometime in 1957-58,[16] represents the decisive moment in the
integration of this reality for Merton.

The section on coinherence in the mystical body, later
in the same chapter, is first altered from TS1 by the omission of five paragraphs on the love of God through others
(V 105-06). Then after a few minor alterations, and a jab
at one of his favorite targets, "self-hypnotism," he once
again stresses the initiative of God in contemplation.

> We enter into possession of God when He invades all
> our faculties with His light and His infinite fire.
> But this business of doping your mind ... merely
> deadens you to all the opportunities for love which
> is the heart of contemplation (V 107).

It is the initiative of God in the lives of contemplatives that gives them a common and dynamic bond with
each other. So, as Merton says, "The more I become identified with God, the more will I be identified with all the
others who are identified with Him" (V 107), not simply
with those who "ressemble Him" (V 107, TS1--spelling à
la française Merton's or, less probably, Sr Thérèse's).
Speaking to his fellow-contemplatives, he asserts that
this means nothing less than "we shall love one another
and God with the same Love with which He loves us and
Himself" (V 108). As he says in Jonas, "His one Image
is in us all, and we discover Him by discovering the
likeness of His Image in one another."[17] In other words,
the identity of human beings with each other in their
creation, their involuntary resemblance to each other because of the existence of the image of God in each and
all of them is less to be stressed than the willed identification which takes place among all of those who find
themselves companions, in God and each other, on the contemplative path towards the full restoration of the likeness of that image to its original, to Christ.

Succeeding paragraphs, which in TS1 exhibit paradox

under stylistic strain, achieve in SC a greater simplicity of expression, yet without the renunciation of mystery (or at the least, mysteriousness). Thus this painful and overstretched statement from TS1 becomes, in SC,
its much more succinct restatement.

> Therefore when I become what I am really meant to
> be I will find out that I am you and you are my
> own self and I am your own self and both of us are
> Christ, both of us are God, and you and I and all
> the millions of others who are one in God are all
> one Life which is the Life of God (V 108, TS1).

> Therefore when you and I become what we are really
> meant to be, we will discover not only that we
> love one another perfectly but that we are the
> same Mystical Person, and that we are both living
> in Christ and Christ in us, and we are all One
> Christ (V 108, SC).

Statements such as "you are my own self and I am your
own self" or "both of us are God" would have offered not
only perplexity but annoyance to Merton's "orthodox
theologian" of the Author's Note (V 12). But the form
of the statement in SC deals with these overstrained
statements in favor of a more modest treatment of the
unity of contemplatives in the mystical body. In SCR,
he will remove the further statement that "we are the
same Mystical Person" and be content to say, with the
New Testament, that "we are all one Christ." The same
process of simplification continues over the next three
paragraphs (V 109); and Merton concludes with a new
section which stresses that this union with other contemplatives on earth is a matter of obscurity, which

can only be realized and enjoyed "in the darkness of
faith" (V 110).

No-one would question this last statement; but where
he goes from there is open to question. He has admitted
that "the silence of contemplation is deep and rich and
endless society, not only with God but with men" (V 110).
Now he controverts himself, and wonders whether it would
not be better if we did not simply forget each other in
contemplation.

> ... perhaps for the time being it is better to
> forget about it, because it might upset our imagi-
> nation. For if we remembered individuals and thought
> of them in our contemplation, that would tend to
> withdraw us from God and therefore from spiritual
> union with them. We remain more truly with them when
> we no longer clearly know them (V 111).

Merton managed to sustain this point of view, surely
that of someone young in the contemplative life, and
nervous about "upsetting" his imagination, through the
publication of SCR; but it is omitted, and the rest of
the paragraph in which it occurs, in NSC. With the human
contact which came to him in his work as teacher and
pastor in the monastery, he simply could not sustain
so bleak a viewpoint. It may also be said that Merton's
use of the word "contemplation" here is imprecise. If
he were referring to unitive contemplation in itself
("the moment of time ... in which he was delivered
into God"--V 478), then he would not in any case have
been able to remember individuals. He is really referring to what may more loosely be called contemplative prayer, the total prayer (including intercession
and the offering of one's life) of a person with a contemplative orientation.

In the meantime, however, after further rewriting
(V 112-15) on the implications of this "true society of
charity" (V 112) in contemplation, he turns to its
ground and correlate in the triune life of God. In TS1
he has already discussed the eternal sharing of love
among the divine Persons, a sharing in which "the Substance of Love makes an infinite escape from selfish-
ness" (V 115-16), and is shared "in the unending pleni-
tude of selfless love" (V 116). As the contemplative
enters more and more into this divine sharing among
"the Three Selves of God" which are "relations of selflessness" (V 118), his own true self emerges. Merton's
use of contemplation as a metaphor of totality, a use
we have already noted, appears again in this context as
he states that the "Love of these Persons is contemplation" (V 118); and for human beings, to share in such
contemplation means to accept a destiny of living "entirely for God and for one another" (in TS1 he had written "for one another and for God"), "as the Persons of
God live for One another" (V 118--in SCR, "in One another").

The next passage of extensive rewriting, that on
the humble man (V 160-63), comprises a foil to the
earlier and rewritten passage on pride (V 83-87). In
TS1, he had somewhat hesitantly posited the view that
it was "not precisely true" (V 160) that, as some believe, humility consists "in being like everybody else";
now he is ready to say quite flatly that "humility consists in being precisely the person you actually are
before God" (V 160). The humble man's individuality is
rooted in God's creation of each of us as different
(see pp. 39-40, above): thus, "since no two people are

alike, if you have the humility to be yourself you will
not be like anyone else in the whole universe" (V 160).
But this individuality will not necessarily appear in
external ways. Rather, it is "something deep in the
soul" (V 161). The truly humble person, the saint, will
not excite himself or herself about the things "that
people licitly[18] eat and drink, wear on their bodies,
or hang on the walls of their houses" (V 161). True
humility operates at a much deeper level, and "brings
with it a deep refinement of spirit" (V 161-62). Even
so, to attempt, under God, to be who one is, may render
a person who is trying to be honest vulnerable to the
accusation of pride. All Merton can counsel is that
"the greatest humility can be learned from the anguish
of keeping your balance in such a position" (V 163).

The last of the major rewritten passages are the
three sections on faith. In them Merton is concerned
to assert the objectivity of faith as "intellectual assent" (V 197) over the vagueness and hyper-subjectivity
which he had encountered in others during his academic
years (cf. V 227), and which in fact he had experienced
himself. Faith, he asserts, is not "a blind sub-conscious
urge towards something vaguely supernatural"; nor is it
"an elemental need in man's spirit," nor a "feeling of
God's existence": in other words, it is "not something
entirely interior and subjective" (V 196). Neither is
it simply an opinion, even an opinion which is "the
fruit of scientific evidence" (V 197), something which
in any case would make it knowledge rather than faith.

In TS1 he had written that "faith is supposed to
perfect the intellect of man and not destroy it" (V 198).
In SC, he expanded on this in asserting the neutrality
to reason of statements of faith, which are accepted as

revealed in the absence of any "natural evidence why they
should be true or why they should be false" (V 198). The
act of faith, however, is quite rational because it is
based on the realization that "our reason can tell us nothing about God as He actually is in Himself" (V 199).
It is the act of faith, in which the contemplative "is
content to know God by loving Him and accepting His
statements about Himself on His own terms" (V 199--in
fact, as conveyed by the magisterium, cf. v 228-31),
which God uses to deliver the contemplative from "the
interminable fluctuation of opinions and theories and
hypotheses upon which no one can agree" (V 199, TS1). In
TS1 this last statement continued into a highly abstract
discussion of the relations of faith, reason and certitude (V 199-201), part of which (V 200) he had already
rejected from the text while still in typescript.

   Having again stressed the "simplicity" of faith,
and having warned the reader not to try to imagine in
any concrete way the entities or assertions to which
faith-statements refer (V 207-08), he concludes his
rewriting in SC of his chapter on faith by holding up
before the contemplative reader the goal of the per-
fecting of faith in contemplation.

   The more perfect faith is, the darker it becomes.
   The closer we get to God, the less is our faith di-
   luted with the half-light of created images and
   concepts. ...

      In this greatest perfection of faith the infi-
   nite God Himself becomes the Light of the darkened
   soul and possesses it entirely with His Truth
   (V 210-11).

There is a parallel in TS1 to each of the sentences in

this last quotation. But now, in SC, Merton adds another
sentence which suggests the possibility of his having
reached a new depth in contemplation since writing the
previous draft. "And at this inexplicable moment the
deepest night becomes day and faith turns into understanding" (V 211). As the years continued, faith remained
an abiding concern. In TS2 it is one of the major themes
to be further revised and amplified.

(c) Smaller Emendations

Throughout the whole process of writing which finally
gave us NSC, Merton made some thousands of minor emendations, in many cases amounting to a change in only one
word. The great majority of these are stylistic only; but
a significant number point to specific developments,
theological and personal. As regards SC, we shall consider these latter alterations under four heads:

    (i) severity of attitude;
   (ii) absolutism of tone;
  (iii) theological concerns; and
  (iv) personal motifs.

(i) Severity of Attitude

In SC, Merton seems to be wobbling back and forth
between impulses which pull him towards a more severe
ascetical position, and others which would move him to
a milder position. In TS1, for example, he had asked how
he could "receive the seeds of freedom if I am not free";
in SC the last phrase has been intensified to "if I am
in love with slavery" (V 29). In TS1 Merton grants that
a person suffering from distractions "may still be praying far better" than someone whose mind "is swimming with
nice clear concepts"; in SC any hint of merit is removed

when he says that such a one "may be forced to pray far
better" (V 358). In TS1 he speaks of the "surest asceti-
cism" in terms (among others) of being "ignored and despised"; in SC this has become "ignored and despised and
forgotten" (V 410); other examples of this can be cited
(cf. V 177, 373, 427). On the other hand, SC also bears
evidence in a number of places of a lessening of this
severity. In SC Merton's question, "Do you think a
saint has to disinfect his interest in created things
...?" has been softened to "excuse his interest" (V 38).
The secret of his identity, first seen as "buried in
the love and mercy of God" is now simply "hidden" there
(V 59). Earlier Merton spoke of freedom from things
that bind one to the "temporal activities and bodily
movements of other men"; in SC, much less obsessionally,
he speaks simply of the "presence of other men" (V 137),
no small reality in the limited living space of an over-
crowded contemplative community, but one in which ob-
sessionality and compulsiveness would only hinder the
contemplative from reaching maturity. Related to this
last instance is his alteration in SC of his rather irri-
table admonition to himself and others not to bother with
men's "intolerable concerns for the way their bodies look
and feel and smell" to the simpler, yet still severe, "look
and feel" (V 140--the whole phrase is omitted in NSC).
Distractions, from being in TS1 a "normal condition" (emphasis Merton's) in the life of prayer, have settled down
in SC to being "often unavoidable" (V 358); and "a planned
campaign of ... strategic mortifications" has in similar
vein been reduced and deflated to "penances" (V 420).
Again, still speaking (as in the previous example) of renunciation, his somewhat melodramatic encouragement to

the reader faced with the challenge of renunciation to
"suffer and grind your teeth and hang on" has been cut
down to "suffer and hang on" (V 420). It is this latter
tendency, however, which will be the dominant one; in
SCR and NSC a number of other lessenings of severity
occur, with no notable alterations in the other direction. Merton by then will have had another decade in
which to mellow.

(ii) Absolutism of Tone
     Absolutism of tone is the stylistic counterpart of
what I have called severity of attitude. More clearly than
the changes considered in the previous section, Merton's
stylistic emendations point in the gentler and more self-
accepting direction which the work will finally evidence.
This tempering takes place by means of moves on Merton's
part from the definite to the indefinite, from the necessary to the possible, or from the superlative to the com-
parative. In two instances only do I note a move in the
other direction. In the first of these, Merton alters "We
do not go up to heaven and find Him" to "We cannot go up
to heaven to find Him" (V 64), a point which is in any
case theologically arguable; and in the second, speaking
of the reaction likely to be elicited from someone attempting to reprove contemplatives unbalanced through overac-
tivity (a big problem for Merton), he changes the nuanced
"they will probably treat you as little short of a heretic" to the flat statement "they will treat you as a heretic" (V 334).

     In the main, however, this group of stylistic altera-
tions achieves a softening of tone. "A man can never enter
into the deepest center of himself" (in contemplation)
becomes "A man cannot enter" (V 106--emphasis Merton's).

The statement that "there is an intense egoism" (in be-
having in a way likely to make oneself popular) becomes
"there can be an intense egoism" (V 159). The assertion
that "people enter monasteries" from inadequate motiva-
tion becomes "people sometimes enter monasteries" (V
164). Merton's conviction that for Catholics to live out
the full implications of the "one true doctrine about
property rights" would mean "that all Christians would
be living with something like the communism of the
first Apostles" is reduced to "most Christians" (V 280).
His sweeping judgement that a man who is almost perfect
in virtue thereby "enters into a dangerous condition of
blindness" to his remaining imperfections becomes the
more realistic "he may enter" (V 422). These are all
small changes; but they contribute to the increase of
moderation and humanness of tone which will mark Merton's
continuing development of the entire work.

(iii) Theological Concerns

       Four interesting (though unrelated) alterations in
SC refine the specifically doctrinal content of TS1. Originally, in the first of these, Merton had said that "theology does not truly begin to be contemplation until we
have transcended the language and separate concepts of
theologians" (V 234). In the second version, he said that
"theology does not truly begin to be theology until ...
etc." It is probable that Merton, in making this change,
was thinking of <u>theologia</u> in patristic usage, to mean
the highest experience of God beyond all thought. If so,
the term "theology" here emphasizes the specific perfection of intellect and understanding in "a single intuition
that unites all dogmas in one simple Light" (V 233), each
particular dogma being a partial refraction of the one

light. Merton may have preferred "theology" here to the
(for him) more inclusive "contemplation" because that term
had become a global metaphor of the totality of human experience and knowing, in God.

In the second, Merton omits the mention of communion
(in the sacramental sense) as a vehicle co-ordinate with
mental prayer in our growth in learning about God (V 304).
Why he should have omitted it is not immediately clear,
inasmuch as he does include a section on the Eucharist
later in the book (V 255-58). In that section, however,
he does say that God's demand for identification with
himself which a sharing in the Eucharist places upon the
mind and heart of the contemplative is "so tremendous
that it ... cannot be expressed" (V 257); and this may
be the reason why the reference to communion was dropped
in the earlier instance. Or, it may be that he was thinking of mental prayer as human activity and the Eucharist
as divine act, from which it might not be seemly for a
contemplative to learn only a "little" (V 304).

In the third, having spoken in TS1 of the night
of the senses as "the night which darkens us and makes
us pure," he speaks in SC of "the night which empties
us" (V 425), thus equating the two dominant terms of apophatic mysticism. In the fourth, he changes the assertion
that God "is the only identity that is there" (V 477) in
the experience of "one who has in ... contemplation vanished into God" (V 476), to the statement that God is
the only one "that acts there"--an alteration which stresses the sovereign activity of God in contemplation and
the passivity, but not absorption, of the contemplative.
This is an alteration which supports some of the emendations in the rewritten passages we have already looked
at.

In addition to these four particular alterations, a
group of changes occur together in his chapter on the
Blessed Virgin Mary. In TS1, he had said that sharing her
"humility and hiddenness and poverty and concealment and
solitude is the only way to know her"; in SC, this becomes
"the best way" (V 264), perhaps because of his recognition
that scripture provides another way, a recognition that
becomes explicit in SCR (V 274). Another change, from "the
voice of God becomes an experience to us in her faith"
to "in her contemplation" (V 266), claims her for the
ranks of the contemplatives, rather than presenting her
simply as a model of faith, something with which the Christian is already well-provided. It perhaps also implies (consistently with Merton's use of the term) that contemplation
includes and requires faith, whereas the reverse is not
necessarily true. Finally, Merton says in TS1 that to be
hidden in the depths of the emptiness of contemplation
is "to share her mission of bringing all men to Him," and
in SC that it is "to share her mission of bringing Him
to all men" (V 273). This shift may have been made to put
the passage into better biblical perspective, in the
sense of a clearer reference to Mary as Theotokos, bearer
of the Incarnate Word, rather than the apostolic role
which the earlier wording suggests. Or it may have been
made to avoid contradicting his earlier comment that
there are certain persons "whom she wills to be hidden
as she is hidden" and who therefore "become great saints
in the sight of God" (V 272), a statement which could
suggest that she fulfills a quasi-soteriological role in
relation to a select or elite group, for which of course
there is no biblical support. Insofar as the Incarnation
as an act of God towards and within the entire human race

carries meaning for all persons, and insofar as Mary
bears a specific role in relation to that act of God,
her significance is, basically, a general one. So it
would seem that Merton, in the second form of his statement, is on safer ground than in the first, which may
have been simply a projection of his early tendency
to generalize very broadly from his own experience. I
mean by this that he may have projected his own strong
sense of connectedness with the Blessed Virgin[19] into a
more general position than he was able to sustain.

(iv) Personal Motifs

The first of these occurs in the chapter on distractions. There Merton had spoken of the most dangerous kind
of distractions, "the ones that draw our will away from
its profound and peaceful occupation with God and involve
it in elaborations of projects that have been concerning
us during our day's work" (V 362). He then went on, in
TS1, to give the following examples: "mental letter writing or the planning of magazine articles or sermons or
speeches or books" (V 363). In SC, he omitted the reference to magazine articles, certainly one of his chief
distractions of the period,[20] probably because it would
have drawn a certain kind of personal attention to him,[21]
or because it would have revealed his situation more
concretely than he wished to do (see also V 385).

A second such motif occurs in Ch. 24 ("Renunciation"), in the opening section. After a discussion in
TS1 of the possibility of the contemplative becoming at-
tached to the poetry of St John of the Cross for reasons
of "poetic pleasure" (V 408), he makes this comment.

What is the good of pretending you have given up
all pleasure if, in fact, you have only renounced

other pleasures in order to take supreme pleasure
in the language and images of The Dark Night of the
Soul?

It may well happen that the true test of your
contemplative vocation may be your willingness to
give up St John of the Cross on the orders of a
director who does not like him and perhaps does not
even appreciate him or understanding him (V 408).
This is a reference to a specific event, recounted by
Merton in a part of The Seven Storey Mountain not included in the published version, but later edited by Sr
Thérèse, and published in Renascence.[22] As in TS1 and SC,
Merton's account occurs in the context of a discussion
on pleasure and renunciation. "I used to love pleasure,"
he begins: "therefore in the monastery I shall have much
discomfort and no pleasure ...."[23] He then mentions that
at the time he was struggling with this dimension of
the contemplative life, he had given up reading particular books to which he thought he was too strongly atta-
ched.

Here I got some help from my new confessor. For
there was one book I would not easily have given up
of my own accord: that was St. John of the Cross.
So the first thing he told me to do was to stop reading St. John of the Cross--in order to see how I
would take it. So for a year or more I did not touch
St. John of the Cross, until he gave me his permission and his blessing and told me it would now be
very desirable that I read St. John of the Cross
again.[24]

By "St. John of the Cross" he means (as we learn from TS1)
The Dark Night of the Soul. In SC, he decided to omit the

first sentence quoted above ("What is the good ...") entirely. In the second sentence he removed the suggestion
that his director (in the excerpt, his confessor) did not
like or appreciate St John of the Cross, leaving, however,
the more serious accusation that he did not understand
the saint, and adding the qualifier that this renunciation
was only "for a time" (V 408). The entire passage is omitted
in SCR, perhaps because he knew that the Renascence article
would soon be published, and thought that his illustration
might be too easily recognized as a personal one.

Another group of references, to women, would also
seem to have some rooting in his personal history. The
most striking of these (although we should make some allow-
ance for the heightened effect of his imperative style)
is his statement in TS1, "Do not complicate your life by
looking at the pictures of their women in magazines," reduced in SC to "the pictures in their magazines" (V 140-41).
Another, in the chapter on detachment, refers to "the un-
bending formalism of these pious men and women"--the words
"and women" being dropped in SC (V 328). Similarly, in
the chapter on religious emotion (Ch. 23, "The Wrong Flame"),
he refers in TS1 to the tears of "children and old ladies"
(V 399-400); in SC the "old ladies" have gone away. In
another place in TS1, where he had addressed his reader
as "my brother or my sister in God" (V 109), the phrase
was dropped entirely when he rewrote the passage for SC.

There is no need to make anything earth-shaking out
of these small changes. From The Seven Storey Mountain,
we know that at Columbia Merton maintained a number of
friendships with women; and from Rice's memoir, we know
of an earlier involvement with a young Englishwoman,
which in Rice's opinion had "a lot to do with his eventual
conversion and vocation."[25] Even in the forties, and to

the end of his life, two of his closest friends and correspondents were women: Naomi Burton Stone, the editor with
whom he had worked on his autobiography, and Sr Thérèse
Lentfoehr. But at this point in his life, the first
months of 1949, these changes, which amount to a virtual
excision of the feminine from SC, signal two realities:
his failure to that point to resolve his sexual or emotional feelings about the women he had known and women
in general,[26] and his life-situation as a male in an
entirely male and celibate society.

(d) Missing Passages

In TS1, as already mentioned, pp. 94, 96-103 and 115-19
are missing from the text as received. Page 94, which occurs towards the end of Ch. 21 ("The Gift of Understanding")
must have dealt with the need for receptivity and poverty
of spirit as the prerequisite for being given the gift of
understanding--to judge, that is, by the equivalent passage which appears in SC (V 375-77). There is no indication in the text of discontinuity; indeed, the opening
words of the passage, from the end of p. 93 of TS1, are
repeated exactly in SC (V 375), and p. 95 goes straight
on from the end of the equivalent to the missing section
(V 377).

The second missing section, pp. 96-103, comprised
the entire text of Ch. 22, called in the list of chapter
headings for TS1 In terra inaquosa (V 5), and in SC "The
Night of the Senses" (V 380-82, 383-92, 393-97). The
chapter in SC is a doctrinally unremarkable but unmis-
takeably Mertonian statement of that phase of contemplative progress in which the absorption of the mind in
the thought of God in obscurity, and the occupation of

the will with a "blind, groping, half-defined desire of
God" (V 393) combine to produce in the contemplative
conditions of darkness and helplessness which make "lucid
and particular acts [of devotion] at once so hard and so
futile" (V 394, cf. 392).

The third missing section, pp. 115-19, comprised
the entire text of Ch 25, called in both TS1 and SC "Inward Destitution" (V 430-40). In SC, the chapter deals
with the contemplative's distaste for his own grossness
of spirit faced with the purity and immensity of God,
or as Merton describes it "the anguish of being helpless
to be anything but what you were not meant to be" (V
431-32), i.e., to be proud and not humble as Merton
has defined that quality: see pp. 73-74 and 78-79, above).
This discussion is balanced, towards the end of the chapter, with a description of the way in which obedience
and acceptance of one's own destitution make it possible
for God to give peace and simplicity of spirit to the
contemplative.

> So it is great praise of God to remain in His si-
> lence and darkness and when we have received this
> gift from Him it would be poor thanks indeed to
> prefer our own dim light and desire some feeling
> of Him that would give us some false and human
> sense of His being (V 439-40).

Altogether, the continuity of the equivalent passages
in SC with the themes and tone of their context in TS1
indicates that in SC we have available to us the basic
substance, if not the entire text, of the originals of
the missing sections as they must once have existed in
TS1. If the originals do reappear, we will have an opportunity to check these speculations and conjectures
against the recovered text.

(e) New Material

There is of course much that is new in the rewritten
passages in SC (see section (b), above). In addition,
however, there are three relatively short sections which
are entirely new in SC. The first of these (V 72-73), one
of the sternest in the work, discusses the disorder of
the natural appetites which is the result of original sin.
Even though man's nature, says Merton, is "good in itself"
(V 72), the reality and power of original sin is such
that there "can be death and impurity in every movement
of natural zeal, even in the ardent love of great perfection" (V 72-73); in SCR this is softened to the statement
that there "can be imperfection even in the ardent love
of great perfection," an indication of Merton's increasing compassion, even so early, for his own human nature
and that of his fellow human beings.[27]

The second passage, to which reference has already
been made, is the magnificent prayer, "Justify my soul,
O God" (V 75-78). Its theme is the total oblation of
self to which God calls the contemplative.

> Let my eyes see nothing in the world but Your glory,
> and let my hands touch nothing that is not for Your
> service. Let my tongue taste no bread that does not
> strengthen me to praise Your glory. I will hear
> your voice and I will hear all harmonies you have
> created ... (V 75).

By the rightly-ordered use of the senses, in other words,
the contemplative glorifies God in every aspect of his
being. But the senses are also capable of the disorder
of sin: and the greater part of the prayer consists of
petitions to be delivered from the well-known "deadly
sins." Lust (V 76), covetousness, envy and sloth (V 77)

are specifically mentioned and their effects described.
Pride, or possibly anger, may be meant by "the death of
deadly sin which puts hell in my soul" (V 76). Avarice
(V 76) would seem to be a doublet for covetousness, possibly in place of gluttony, against which the monastic
regimen of Gethsemani was more than sufficient protect-
ion. The prayer concludes with a petition for love.

> Occupy my whole life with the one thought and the
> one desire of love, that I may love not for the
> sake of merit, not for the sake of perfection, not
> for the sake of virtue, not for the sake of sanc-
> tity, but for love alone (V 77-78).

The final words of this paragraph will be changed twice
after this--from "love alone" to "God alone" in SCR,
and finally in NSC to "You alone." Merton's strongly
personalist spirituality could not rest content in abstraction at this point, even the abstraction of love.

The third element of new material (V 92-97, 98-100)
concerns coinherence in the mystical body, and occurs
earlier in the same chapter ("We Are One Man") which
contains the extensively-rewritten passage on the same
subject discussed in section (b), above. The saints
love sanctity, Merton begins,

> not because it separates them from the rest of us
> and places them above us, but because, on the con-
> trary, it brings them closer to us and in a sense
> places them below us. Their sanctity is given them
> in order that they may help us and serve us ...
> (V 93).

Humility enables the saints to preserve their right relation to others in the body of Christ, preventing them
from building up their own idea of themselves by despi-
sing others, and so maintaining their holy union with

each other. Yet even "the professionally holy, and sometimes the holy most of all, can waste their time in com-
petition with each other, in which nothing is found but
misery" (V 97). But growth in the Spirit for faithful contemplatives will mean the accepting of an ability, as a
gift from God, "to exult in the virtues and goodness of
others more than they ever could have done in their own"
(V 99).

*

When <u>Seeds</u> <u>of</u> <u>Contemplation</u> was published in March
of 1949, it was already, as demonstrated in this chapter,
a work which had undergone extensive revision and development, by subtraction, by rewriting, by emendation and by
addition. Like its predecessor, TS1, it could still be
called severe and absolutist, still narrowly rather than
generously Catholic and Christian. But as its author ma-
tured in his vocation, he began a process of tempering
and expansion of spirit. The first effects of this maturing, at least in relation to the work we are studying,
we have seen as we have carefully examined the text of
<u>Seeds</u>. This maturing process was to have its final ex-
pression (in terms of this work) some thirteen years later
with the publication of the term of that process, <u>New</u>
<u>Seeds</u>.

CHAPTER 5

SCR: SEEDS REVISED

Whatever his misgivings as recorded in The Sign of
Jonas (the favorable reviews may have helped), Seeds
went into a revised edition at the time of the seventh
printing, on 19 December 1949.[1] A British revised edition was published in 1950, and went into at least three
printings, the latest in 1956. In the American edition,
it comprises five leaves unpaginated, pp. xi-xvi of front
and prefatory matter, the text proper on pp. 1-191, and
one blank leaf at the end. Measuring 21.5 by 13.5 cm, it
was bound, according to Frank Dell'Isola's bibliography,
in an off-white sackcloth, one copy only of which I have
seen.[2] However, it was also published in a brown linen
binding, not mentioned by Dell'Isola, a copy of which I
own: the text in both bindings is of course identical.
In the variorum, the text is that of the original printing.

No reviews are recorded in the usual sources, no
excerpts from it were pre-published, and Merton makes
no reference to it in The Sign of Jonas. Four brief excerpts were later published in an anthology of contemplative writings.[3] It later appeared in a paperback edition, published by Dell on 22 September 1953. Measuring
16 by 11 cm, the paperback comprised 189 pages and one
blank leaf. It omitted the table of contents and the
frontispiece found in all the bound editions.

The revised edition is the least-known of the pub-

lished versions. Many bibliographies do not mention it,
and most critics do not distinguish in citation between
SC and SCR. Beyond my own studies, only those of Shannon,
Woodcock and Sr Thérèse refer to the revision.[4] Sr Thérèse
may even be referring to a further (projected) revision
still, when in her overview of Merton's writings she gives
summer 1950 as a time when Merton was preparing a "second
edition" of Seeds.[5] In that reference she quotes from a
letter from Merton to herself dated 28 August 1950, making
it unlikely that she is mistaken as to the date. So it may
be that as early as 1950 Merton saw SCR as in need of
further revision yet.

With translations now made into 14 languages, Seeds
Revised (together with New Seeds) has been more often
translated than any other work of Merton's (the Mountain
comes close with 13). In 1951 it was translated into German and Italian; in 1952 into Danish, Dutch, French and
Spanish; in 1954 into Swedish and Flemish (a Belgian edition of the Dutch); in 1955 into Portuguese; in 1959 into
Chinese; in 1960 into a Latin-American Spanish as part of
the projected Argentinian collection of Merton's works;
in 1965 into Japanese; and in 1966 into Vietnamese and
again into Japanese. Translations have also been made
into Korean, Polish and again into Swedish.[6]

*

Published only nine months after SC, SCR incorporates
more than 150 smaller or larger textual changes. To the
"Author's Note" at the beginning of SC, Merton now added
a "Preface to the Revised Edition" (V 6-7). In it he recognized that the book had already proved popular, and ex-

pressed both his happiness and his embarrassment at the
fact. He continued to assert the unconnected character
of his reflections, and admitted the inclusion in his
writing of "expressions that might prove to be too loose
for the literal-minded" (V 6), some of which--as a service
to the not-so-literal-minded--we pointed out in the last
chapter. The revision he describes in a somewhat under-
stated way as "a few minor corrections" (V 6). He then
warns the reader not to expect a systematic treatise, but
rather one in which

> the author is talking about spiritual things from
> the point of view of experience rather than in the
> concise terms of dogmatic theology or of metaphy-
> sics. In religion, as in the natural life, the lan-
> guage of experience and the language of dogma or
> science may find themselves opposed. Although
> everybody is well aware that the sun does not rise,
> we say that it rises .... So, too, in the mystical
> life ... we tend to speak of the soul being "anni-
> hilated" in the experience of God .... This is not
> meant to be taken as a literal scientific state-
> ment, any more than we mean to be taken literally
> when we say the "sun rises" (V 7).

Reinforcing his statement that he is writing from the
point of view of experience is his further comment that
although his concerns in the book have been expressed
"better already by the saints," he has tried to say them
"in the language of the men of our time" (V 7); and he
thenconcludes by repeating his submission of all his
writing to the Church's teaching authority.

Following the patternof the last chapter, we shall
consider SCR under these heads:

(a) omitted passages;

(b) smaller emendations; and

(c) new material (in addition to the "Preface").

(a) Omitted Passages

A number of passages would seem to have been omitted
in SCR simply because they are repetitive. Among these
are passages on the Trinity (V 116), the gift of interior
light in contemplation (V 207), and the use of methodical
forms of meditation (V 394). To these we may add three
related passages on the role of images, especially those
pertaining to the humanity of Christ (V 242-43, 244, 248),
omitted in the course of Merton's attempt to reconcile
his own lack of need for them and his at the time rather
reluctant admission that others found them useful and
even necessary.[7]

In another place (V 441-42), he omits a passage
dealing with the phenomenon that some of the saints seem
not to have known "this highest joy" (V 441) of contemplation because of their devotion to "the love and the active service of other men" (V 442). But no sooner has he
advanced this position than he feels himself required to
refute his own suggestion that the love of God in God
can be divided from the love of God in others. It had
been retained in SC unchanged from TS1; its omission in
SCR may simply have been his decision not to raise an
issue which he would end by declaring it a non-issue, a
decision very much in keeping with some of the mitiga-
tions which we shall shortly be noting. Linked to this
omission may be two others, one a reference to "our own
coarse nature" (V 445), the other a slam at "the erratic
enthusiasm of a human friendliness and a human instinct
for communication" (V 454)--clearly a self-reproach.

These excisions have a common effect, that of softening,
lightening and humanizing the revision, an effect in
which they are supported by many of the smaller emendations.

One other omission, very significant both for the
tone and perspective of the final text in NSC (as indeed
for much of Merton's later work), is perhaps his single
most important change in SCR. The sentence in question
is one of the sternest and most tendentious passages in
TS1. It is probably Merton's most extreme statement in
that text to do with Catholic teaching as such, and represents, in my view, the point of farthest distance
away from the interest in Asian religion which marked
both his academic life in the late thirties and his
later monastic life at Gethsemani. In TS1 and SC, this
sentence had followed the statement that the saints arrived at the deepest knowledge of God through the tradition of prayer guarded and fostered by the magisterium.

> For outside the magisterium directly guided by
> the Spirit of God we find no such contemplation
> and no such union with Him--only the void of nir-
> vana or the feeble intellectual light of Platonic
> idealism or the sensual dreams of the Sufis (V 229).

It could not have been the exception taken to this passage by Merton's lone recorded British reviewer of
Seeds, as I had earlier suggested, which caused him to
omit it in SCR; as that reviewer had remarked, it was
because SC was "in other respects a generous book that
this passage strikes so false a note."[8] But SCR, as
I later realized, was published four days before the
British review, which appeared on 23 December 1949.
In the event, as we know, it was a note which Merton
chose not to sustain, coming in time, and in keeping

with his own generous nature, to an affirming and inclusi-
vist (but not syncretist) view of inter-religious contact,
the fullest accounts of which may be found in his Asin
Journal. Merton's explicit interest in Asian spiritualities during his monastic years is usually dated from the
late fifties, and his sending of his book The Wisdom of
the Desert to D. T. Suzuki, interpreter-in-chief of Zen
to the western world.[9] So it is interesting to see him,
as early as 1949, making this particular omission in SCR.
Autobiographically considered, his purpose in making the
statement in the first place was very likely far less a
theological one (although without doubt he believed the
propositional truth of his own words) than it was an existential one, conveying his joy in having found religious
security and a firm base for an integrated spiritual life,
as contrasted with his desultory encounters with Platonism
at Oakham[10] and with Asian religion at Columbia.[11] Here
he does what later he says there is no point in doing--
affirming himself as a Catholic "by denying all that is
Muslim, Jewish, Protestant, Hindu, Buddhist, etc."[12] However, as a result of the reading and research which he
did after his recovery in 1950, Merton felt free to re-
develop an interest in and respect for these spiritual
traditions other than his own. His personal integration
of Catholic faith and tradition had brought him to a
much less aggressive and self-conscious assertion of his
position as a Christian than we find expressed in this
omitted sentence. By the time of the publication of NSC,
indeed, he was deeply into Zen, which is represented
ikonically on the last page of that book by the old frog
heard by the Japanese poet Bashō.[13] The emptiness (in
the apophatic sense) created for NSC by the omission of

this passage in SCR had opened a way for Bashō's frog
to splash out a humorous Mertonian apology for his dismissal of the non-Christian traditions.

(b) Smaller Emendations

As in SC, so in SCR Merton made a large number of
minor alterations. Here we shall group them and consider
them under these heads:

    (i) severity of attitude;
   (ii) absolutism of tone;
  (iii) the language of personalism;
   (iv) the description of the divine; and
    (v) the "spiritual put-down."

(i) Severity of Attitude

In SC, Merton had gone back and forth between increasing and decreasing the severity of his ascetical attitudes. In SCR, however, this vacillation has ceased and
all the alterations in attitude are consistently in the
direction of tempering. One notably concrete example
concerns newspapers. In TS1 and SC, Merton had bidden his
readers to avoid the places of amusement where people
gather "to cheat and insult one another," and had added,
"Do not read their newspapers, if you can help it" (V 140).
In SCR, the statement about cheating and insulting was
maintained, but the remark about the newspapers was miti-
gated. "Do not read their newspapers unless you are
really obliged to keep track of what is going on. Newspapers are a penance, not a diversion" (V 140). During
his time of sickness (1949-50), Merton, while in hospital, had been given permission to read newspapers. which
may account for his milder comment in SCR.[14] By the time
of NSC, he is no longer willing to include them in this

context, although his attitude was still to some extent
negative. However, by 1961 he had become aware of the negative effects of advertizing,[15] and so added the brief
admonition, "Do not read their advertisements" (V 141--
British spelling Merton's).

Numerous small alterations continue this process of
tempering. In TS1 and SC, Merton had said that the saint
is "scandalized at no man's sin." In spite of the intended
negation, however, the use of the word "scandalized" suggested something of the opposite, which Merton recognized
when in SCR he says that the saint "judges no man's sin"
(V 42). In a reference to money, one might now find joy
by "giving it all away" rather than by "throwing it away"
(V 282). A reference to the "intensity of zeal" with which
a contemplative, in an imperfect way, may seek perfection,
is qualified as the "intensity of self-conscious zeal"
(V 329); zeal as such is rehabilitated. God is said to
perfect our faculties, in the darkness of contemplation,
by seeming to "defeat and destroy all their activity"--
thus TS1 and SC; in SCR he is said simply to "defeat all
their activity" (V 345). And of a man in the night of
the senses, carried away with fear or impatience, Merton's
later statement--"he will come to a standstill"--is, even
as it stands, more hopeful than his earlier one: "everything is lost" (V 387).

(ii) Absolutism of Tone

This tempering of attitude in SCR, unlike SC, is now
consistently supported by a relativization of many statements. The flat statement in TS1 and SC that we "do not
yet love God" becomes the more mellow comment that we "do
not yet perfectly love God" (V 45); similarly, Merton's

comment on the communion of all contemplatives in the
sharing of their call--"this communion belongs only to
heaven"--is softened in SCR by the qualifier "perfect"
before "communion" (V 454). The judgement that "Some of
the most virtuous men in the world are also the bitter-
est and most unhappy" becomes the more balanced "Sometimes virtuous men are also bitter and unhappy" (V 95),
in recognition that, realistically, human beings are not
so simple as to be either happy or unhappy all the time.
The assertion that the one "who is not stripped and poor
and naked within his own soul will always unconsciously
do the works he has to do for his own sake" is cooled by
the removal of "always" (V 96). Another confident assertion, that those who are enthralled by the "theology"
of the devil smack their lips over the prospect of the
end of the world "because they derive a deep, subcon-
scious comfort from the thought that many other people
will fall into the hell which they themselves are going
to escape" is modified to "Perhaps this is because ..."
(V 151). Of a person led by God into the darkness where
contemplation is found, the more temperate "you are not
able to rest in the false sweetness of your own will"
replaces the absolutist "you will never be able" (V 311);
and in a context in which Merton describes the poten-
tially anaesthetic effect of a book used for meditation,
the phrase "probably ruined it" replaces the bleaker
"ruined it altogether" (V 359).

(iii) The Language of Personalism
    In SCR Merton makes a number of changes which
clarify his personalist terminology, and prepare for its
refinement in NSC. Thus for the phrase "This Love is a
Person," he substitutes "This Love is God Himself"; and

for the statement that "we are the same Mystical Person,"
he substitutes "we are both living in Christ and Christ
in us" (V 108). A reference to "the one Person of all the
elect" in SC becomes "the One Body and Soul of all the e-
lect" in SCR (and finally "the one Body of all the elect"
in NSC: V 109). Similarly, "the mystical Person of Christ
in the earlier versions becomes "the Mystical Christ" in
SCR (V 113, cf. 119); and "one Person" becomes "One" (V
119). In a reference to the Trinity, the words "The Love
of these Persons" becomes "The interior life of God" (V
118). Finally, the innocent of this world, earlier said
to be "one Person in Him" are simply called "one in Him"
(V 123).

These changes are made, not from any hesitation
about the use of the Chalcedonian term "person" in reference to Father, Son or Spirit, but in a way which fore-
shadows its development in NSC. This development takes
place there in language which comes from Maritain, by
means of the terms "person" (hence, conjecturally, the
changes in SCR) and "individual,"[16] used in elaboration
of Merton's terms "true self" and "false self," terms
basic to the theological anthropology of TS1, SC and
SCR. In TS2 and NSC, the "person" is the "deep transcendent self that awakens only in contemplation," "the
hidden and mysterious person in whom we subsist before
the eyes of God" (V 19). It is "above all the human
person" (V 62, emphasis Merton's) which is the object of
God's saving activity, rather than humanity in the abstract. This person is the "true inner self" (V 464),
hidden both from "the world" and the "false self," pos-
sessing "neither biography nor end" (V 465); for it is
sustained by God's love in contemplation. By contrast,

the "individual" is "at best the vesture, the mask, the
disguise of that mysterious and unknown 'self' whom most
of us never discover until we are dead" (V 19). It is
"superficial ... not eternal, not spiritual ... utterly
frail and evanescent" (V 20), "the smoke-self that must
inevitably vanish" (V 63). The fuller dimension of this
development we will trace in section (b) of Chapter 6,
below. Here we will simply record that to the smaller
changes of this kind already noted in SCR, Merton adds
the following refinements in NSC. "For "our natural
selves" he substitutes simply "people" (V 52); for "person," "character" (V 72); and for "themselves," "their
external selves" (V 100)--in these instances redeeming
"self" as well as "person" from its occasionally vague
usage in TS1, SC and SCR.

(iv) The Description of the Divine

A further set of changes in SCR concerns the language
in which the divine "activity" (no term is adequate) is
described. In various contexts Merton says that love never ceases to "rest in" rather than "return to" the Holy
Spirit (V 117); and that our destiny is to live "in" God
and "in" one another as the divine Persons live "in" one
another rather than "for" one another (V 118). In other
passages he omits words like "circulation" (V 117, two
occurrences) and "returned" (V 117, cf. 118), and the
phrase (implying movement) "to one another" (V 118). The
effect of these changes is a unified one, directed towards a describing of God (the inadequacy of all language, including these "improvements," admitted[17]) as one
in whom motion is rest, and who in changing never changes.
In NSC Merton builds on this beginning by refining other
terms for God's activity in the direction of intimacy and

concreteness. Thus for "the radius of God's will" he substitutes "the reach of God's will" (V 57); for "essence,"
"mystery" (V 102--a philosophical term replaced with a
biblical one); and for "dominates" (as expressing God's
relation to the believer's contemplation", "is the source
of" (V 396). These are tiny changes indeed; and yet the
care with which Merton makes them testifies to his continuing penetration of the reality of God, simultaneously
motionless and active, far away and very close, transcendent and immanent, beyond all the dualities in the
paradoxical reality of divine life.

(v) The "Spiritual Put-Down"

A final and notable genre of emendation is that of
the omission of the "spiritual put-down," which for the
contemporary reader mars a complete enjoyment of TS1 and
SC. In SCR Merton begins to renounce its use, and continues to do so in NSC. The genre will be recognized from
such examples as these.

On mystical union:

> This is the way mystical union appears in the
> minds of those who have no idea of what it
> really is (V 288, SC).

> This is the way mystical union appears in the
> minds of those who do not realize that the
> essence of that union is a pure and selfless
> love ... (V 288, SCR).

On the saints:

> Do you think they walked around with faces like
> stones and did not listen to the voices of men
> ... or understand the joys and sorrows of those
> who were around them? Then you do not know what

contemplation is (V 38, TS1 and SC; second sentence omitted in SCR).
On God's use of the natural instincts:
> ... be careful not to get in His way with your
> own innate Rotarian instinct for companionship
> (V 455, SCR; "Rotarian" omitted in NSC--cf. the
> excisions on V 445 and 454).

On the two natures of Christ:
> If you have discovered some kind of contempla-
> tion that gives you only one without the other,
> you are a heretic (V 239; omitted in NSC).

The brief passage omitted in SCR on V 290-91 is milder in
tone, but belongs to the same class of comment.

The spiritual put-down is identified by the use of
a rhetorical question, the answer to which is an indication of the ignorance of the one questioned; by spiritual
name-calling ("you are a heretic"); or by a current of
self-accusation which comes between writer and reader on
the feeling level. Anyone familiar with Guigo's Meditationes (one of the ancestors of Seeds, according to Merton)
will recognize that "the one questioned" is usually Merton himself; but this is not always immediately apparent.
One reviewer saw these "angry little jabs" in SC as revealing in their author "a man of flesh and blood."[18] I
prefer to interpret Merton's deletion of them, beginning
in SCR and continuing in NSC, as a sign, not of flesh-and-
bloodlessness, but of increased self-acceptance and self-
oriented compassion, of flesh more and more ruled by
spirit. Certainly this view is supported by the current
of self-deprecation found in Jonas, and its virtual absence from the later journal, Conjectures.

Finally, one notable non-alteration in SCR may be
mentioned. In SC Merton had written, in a passage on the

Eucharist: "I write this without being yet a priest because
I have known it to some degree merely by kneeling by the
altar as server" (V 256). Between the publication of SC
and SCR, Merton had been ordained to the priesthood at
Gethsemani (on 26 May 1949);[19] so it is curious that in
SCR he did not amend this passage accordingly. I can only
wonder if in a curious way this also was not some sort of
self-put-down, an unwillingness, at this point, to claim
for himself the honor of the priesthood.

(c) New Material

In addition to the preface to SCR (V 6-7), there
are two groups of passages new in the revision. The first,
of very loosely related items, concerns what may be termed
the "imperfections of the holy ones." In the first of the
passages within this grouping (V 97-98), Merton gives il-
lustrations of how "saints did not always agree with
saints" (V 97), among them Peter and Paul, as well as Philip Neri and Charles Borromeo: "And sometimes very holy
men have been very exasperating people and very tiresome
to live with" (V 97). But God, in Merton's view, permitted them to retain these "defects and imperfections and
blind-spots and eccentricities" (V 98), in order to keep
their basic sanctity hidden from them, and thereby made
it possible for them to be "polished and perfected by
trial and persecution ... from the people they lived
with" (V 98, cf. 95, 97). It is notable here that Merton
is not about to lower his view of his vocational goal:
it is the imperfection of the saints that he is concerned
with. Lax's comment of years before is still burning in
hsi memory; all he is doing with his increasingly realistic observations of community life is making them serve

this long-held goal of personal sanctity.

The second of these passages (V 138-39) deals with
the resistance to interior solitude on the part of some
of the "professionally pious" (V 97). They are "men dedicated to God whose lives are full of restlessness" (V
138), whose "lives are devoured by activities and strang-
led with attachments" (V 139). The passage is classic,
and deserves quotation in extenso as vintage Merton.

> Interior solitude is impossible for them. They fear
> it. They do everything they can to escape it. What
> is worse, they try to draw everyone else into acti-
> vities as ceaseless and as devouring as their own.
> ... They love to organize meetings and banquets and
> conferences and lectures. They print circulars,
> write letters, talk for hours on the telephone in
> order that they may gather a hundred people together
> in a large room where they will all fill the air
> with smoke and make a great deal of noise and roar
> at one another and clap their hands and stagger
> home at last patting one another on the back with
> the assurance that they have all done great things
> to spread the Kingdom of God (V 139).

To be dedicated to God is not enough to guarantee that
one will honor the spirit of interior solitude. Here he
portrays its opposite, the spirit of the backroom, at its
task of degrading contemplative hearts. Doubtless he is
calling on his memory of Columbia days in the details of
this description; but that he included it in a work such
as this after eight years in the monastery suggests that
he discerned the presence of this pernicious spirit
within Gethsemani itself, once so romanticized. (As someone who continues to struggle with this incubus myself,
I beat my institutional breast at how immediately it ap-

plies to some of us outside the cloister.)

The third such passage concerns the degree of poverty appropriate to a monastery. In TS1 and SC, Merton had shared his conviction that it

> is good for a monastery to be poor. It is good for the monks to have to be content with clothes that are worn very thin and covered with patches and to get worse food than the Rule allows ... (V 414-15).

But in SCR he feels the need to qualify the extravagant tone of this point of view.

> However, there is a limit beyond which poverty in a monastery ought not to go. ... And though it may be good for a monastery to be poor, the average monk will not prosper spiritually in a house where the poverty is really so desperate that everything else has to be sacrificed to manual labor and material cares (V 415).

Taken together, these passages bear witness to Merton's increasing realism about life in the monastery (but little recognition of what poverty means for the involuntarily poor), and they suggest the plausibility, even the inevitability, of his shift of interest towards society beyond the monastery. His first image of the monastery, gleaned from the Catholic Encyclopaedia, was very romantic,[20] and his romanticism was fuelled to blazing heat by his first visit to Gethsemani.

> ... this church ... is the real capital of the country in which we are living. This is the center of all the vitality that is in America. This is the cause and reason why the nation is holding together.[21]

In Jonas this romanticism reached its plateau, although

Merton continued to celebrate there the minutiae of monastic observance with considerable flourish. So perhaps these
passages, new in SCR, give testimony to the birth of the
realism which by the time of Conjectures was fully and
matter-of-factly expressed. On the one hand, there is no
doubt of his deep affection for the monastic family of
his own profession, or of his intention to be a monk of
Gethsemani until death.[22] On the other hand, by the time
of Conjectures (written 1956-65, during Merton's forties)
he is quite ready to engage in criticism both trenchant
and loyal of what he now regards as a marginal institution within western society.[23]

The second loose grouping of passages new in SCR
concerns the place of images in contemplative (or perhaps
pre-contemplative) prayer. The first of these passages
(V 244-45) occurs in Ch. 13 ("Through a Glass"). In the
part of the chapter preceding the new insert, Merton had
contrasted those for whom "it is quite easy to return
within themselves and find a simple picture of Christ in
their imagination" with others who, if they try to emulate
these first ones, will only "fill their heads with problems
and disturbances that make prayer impossible" (V 243): and
it is clear from the context that his sympathy is with the
latter. For them, "the indistinct, unanalyzed notion of
Christ is enough to keep their faith fully occupied in a
simple awareness of Him Who is really present in our souls
by His Divinity" (V 243). The new passage takes off from
the mention of this "simple awareness" and argues the case
for the superiority of non-imaginal to imaginal prayer.

> This loving awareness is a thing more real and more
> valuable by far than anything we can arrive at by
> our interior senses alone: for the picture of Jesus
> we may have in our imagination remains nothing but

> a picture, while the love that His grace produces
> in our hearts can bring us into direct contact with
> Him as He really is (V 244-45).

The function of images, as Merton presents it, is entirely
preparatory to "a more intimate contact with Him by love"
(V 245). A late article, from which we have already quoted,
gives us his mature resolution of this theme, which he
settles to his own satisfaction by stressing that it is
in the risen-ness of Christ that the Christian contemplative finds the terminus of contemplation, while at the
same time it is his humanity through which we approach
his divinity.

> ... the mysteries of Christ's human life on earth
> can become the object of our admiration and our
> love. But they are not, strictly speaking, the
> ultimate resting-place of contemplation, which is
> a light received in the inner depths of our being
> from the risen Saviour, God and Man, reigning in
> the glory of the Father.[24]

This is basically what he was saying in SCR; but mixed
in with this earlier recognition of the legitimate place
of images is a certain testiness with those whose need
to rely on their imaginations lasted longer than his own.
And so he reluctantly concludes, almost tangibly turning
his back on the discussion and leaving the more image-
oriented contemplatives to their own devices.

> ... when His love begins to burn within us, there
> is surely no strict necessity for using our imagina-
> tions any more. Some may like to, some may not, and
> others may have no choice. Use whatever helps you,
> and avoid what gets in your way (V 245, cf. the
> passage omitted, V 242-43).

Another new passage, also dealing with the imagination in
prayer (V 392-93), develops his statement in SC that meditation and affective prayer should be given up "if they
simply deaden and exhaust the mind and will, and fill them
with disgust" (V 392). That the imagination is giving to
the contemplative "no more pleasure and no more fruit"
(V 393) is the well-known indication that it is time to
give up active meditation, and to let the absorption of
mind and will in the obscurity of God introduce one to
the peace which grows "in blindness and darkness" (V 394),
to the peace which passes all understanding and all
feeling. In saying this, of course, Merton is working the
very center of the mystical mainstream, and no later nu-
ancing will be necessary.

*

Essentially, TS1, SC and SCR share a common structure
and cover common ground. But beginning, however haltingly,
in SC, and continuing in SCR, there is a more and more noticeable shift of tone and, to a lesser extent, of theological and ascetical stance. SCR remained, in my judgement, Merton's operative basic statement[25] on the contemplative life for a decade and more. But the years 1949 to
1961 were to bring enormous changes in attitude and areas
of concern, shifts vitally reflected in TS2 and NSC. These
changes are without doubt extensive enough to justify the
"New" in the title of the final text; and to an examination of the amplifications and additions (and to a much
lesser degree, deletions) of these last two documents of
our study we now turn.

CHAPTER 6

TS2: AMPLIFICATIONS AND ADDITIONS

After the publication of SCR, Merton waited another
decade before turning once again to the work of revision.
The first indication we have of his intention to revise
is found in another letter to Sr Thérèse.

> ... I think I may do a rather thorough piece of re-
> vision on Seeds of Contemplation, a new edition is
> called for. I thought of this when I got a letter
> from a man in Pakistan who is an authority on Su-
> fism and realized I couldn't send him the book
> because of an utterly stupid remark I had made
> about the Sufi.[1]

In fact (see pp. 99-101, above), Merton had omitted this
sentence in SCR (V 229). Had he remembered this, he
could have sent a copy to his Pakistani correspondent.
In any case, we should be grateful for this lapse of
memory, which stirred him into the reworking of SCR
which eventually resulted in the publication of New Seeds.

The revision was carried out sometime between the
date of his letter to Sr Thérèse (5 December 1960) and
10 April 1961, the date of the imprimatur given by the
abbot general of the Cistercians (V 2). TS2, the record
of the major part of this revision, consists of 80 sheets
of white, unlined looseleaf paper, eight-and-one-half
by eleven inches, punched with three holes, and bound in
a plastic looseleaf binder. Together with TS1, it forms
part of the Merton collection at Columbia.

TS2 is a different kind of document than the other
four, each of which comprises (or, in the case of TS1,
originally comprised) a complete book. It contains some
nine-tenths of the material which appears for the first
time in NSC, and was originally written by Merton as a
series of inserts into the text of SCR, either as amplifications of existing themes or as additional material
on new aspects of his subject. Its 80 sheets contain 89
pages of text: 66 typed pages, most bearing holograph
emendation; 21 pages entirely in holograph; and two
typed pages by a person unknown, in French, probably
the report of a publisher's reader (this last what I
have called in the variorum TS2a). The 87 pages of TS2
proper contain 37 major inserts, each of which is carried
forward into NSC. Insert 1 contains the new preface and
Chs. 1 and 2 of NSC ("What is Contemplation?" and "What
Contemplation is Not"). In their own sequence, the
other inserts are numbered as follows: 2, 4-9, 9a, 10-20,
20a, 21-34, and the final insert, Ch. 39, "The General
Dance." There is no insert 3, and there is no element in
the text of NSC which might be a missing insert. Between
inserts 2 and 4 in the variorum there are only two partial entries (V 29) and one new sentence (V 30), neither
of which is what Merton would have called an insert. Each
insert is headed with its own number and a reference to
the page of SCR into the text of which it was to be inserted; these headings are all given in the variorum.
When I received it, TS2 was out of order in relation to
NSC. I therefore paginated it as received, in case the
order in which it had been arranged should later prove
to have some significance.[2]

*

The eleven years between the publication of SCR and
the time when Merton began work on the amplifications and
additions which TS2 contains were, for him, years of extensive reading and writing, and perhaps more importantly
for the shape and tone of what was to be published as
NSC, years of renewed contact with people, both in and
out of the order, of all faiths and none. This contact
was both more varied and more intimate than anything he
had experienced since entering Gethsemani in 1941. In the
new preface, he refers to the purpose of the revision--
"to say many new things that could profitably be added
to the old" (V 8)--in the light of the changes those
years had brought.

> When the book was first written, the author had no
> experience in confronting the needs and problems
> of other men. The book was written in a kind of iso-
> lation, in which the author was alone with his own
> experience of the presence of God. And such a book
> can be written best, perhaps only, in solitude.
> The second writing[3] has been no less solitary than
> the first: but the author's solitude has been modi-
> fied by contact with other solitudes: with the lone-
> liness, the simplicity, the perplexity of novices
> and scholastics of his monastic community: with the
> loneliness of people outside any monastery; with
> the loneliness of people outside any Church ... (V 8).

He acknowledges the unexpected popularity of SC (to which
we may link SCR), then describes his revised intention.
The new book which would be realized when TS2 was incor-
porated into SCR, and when the alterations and additions
of NSC had been added, was not intended for everybody.

It is not intended for all religious people. It is

not addressed primarily to Catholics, though it
should be clear that the author has tried, in
every case, to explain difficult matters in language that accords with Catholic theology (V 9).
One reviewer of SC had criticized Merton for not acknowledging the validity of spiritualities other than his
own, and for presenting his own treatment of a traditional spirituality, both implicitly and explicitly,
as alone authoritative.[5] However, his perspective in
TS2 (and NSC) is decidedly pluralist. "There are very
many religious people who have no need for a book like
this, because theirs is a different kind of spirituality"
(V 9). Beyond the Roman Catholic, ecumenical-Christian,
or even formally inter-religious orbits there will be,
he hopes, "people without formal religious affiliations
who will find in these pages something that appeals to
them. If they do, I am glad, as I feel myself a debtor
to them more than to the others" (V 9-10). If the "others"
are the "very many religious people" to whom he has already referred, then Merton is acknowledging here a deep
indebtedness to persons without institutional or formal
membership in religious bodies. If this is so, it is difficult to know exactly to whom this statement refers.[6]
In any case, he continues to write as a Catholic, but as
a Catholic whose membership in the human race has come
to mean much more to him than it did at the time of the
writing of SC and SCR.[7] Still, the elemental affirmations
of the earlier versions are all found in TS2 (and NSC):
the call to contemplation as the prime means towards the
discovery of the true self; the need for continued watch-
fulness towards society in its capacity to be the ally
of the false self; and the meditations on the love, will
and purpose of God.

But his statement in SC, repeated in NSC, that "there
is no attempt at apologetics" (V 12), is belied by the
large amount of patently apologetic material in TS2. Much
of it is related to themes already present in the earlier
versions; much, however, is new. It was included by Merton in TS2 either because he felt that a theme presented
in the earlier versions needed to be balanced or redeve-
loped, or because it represented an area of increased interest for him, an area which he wanted to integrate more
fully into his general approach to the spiritual life.
Topics to which he devotes brief treatments are (among
others) the knowledge of God's will (V 27-29, 34-35, 128-
29); creation (V 36-37, 39-41); solitude (V 88-89, 90-92);
control of the appetites (V 141-43, 146-47); the person
of Christ in prayer (V 239-41, 250-51, 269-61); and the
monastic virtues of obedience and poverty (V 313-17, 411-
12). Although interesting, these topics are less important than those to which Merton gives more space, and we
will not consider them here. But we will have a good
grasp of the areas in which he saw a need for major re-
development if we consider the material contained in
TS2 which deals with

   (a) contemplation;
   (b) the self;
   (c) humankind divided: and
   (d) faith.

(a) Contemplation
   In his new preface, Merton acknowledged that the very
word "contemplation" had proved problematic to some, "almost a magic word, or if not magic, then inspirational,
which is almost as bad" (V 8). In the two chapters newly-

written for the beginning of the new edition and in the
final insert (in NSC, Ch. 39), he therefore attempts to
solve this problem of rescuing contemplation[8] from an
elitist[9] fate by laicizing and humanizing his way of
speaking of it, and by offering it to his readers not as
a "spiritual commodity" (V 8, cf. 291-93), but as an experiential grasp of reality, beyond all dualities, through
which the contemplative person lives his or her life.
Neither of the two initial chapters ("What is Contemplation?" and "What Contemplation is Not") restricts itself
to the topic suggested by its title. It is true that in
the first, Merton does take a generally cataphatic approach, and in the second, an apophatic approach. But
the language of cataphasis and apophasis is mingled
throughout them as paradoxical testimony to the necessity
of balancing each with the other, and of not waiting so
long to do so that an unbalanced impression begins to form
in the mind of the reader. Thus, in the following statement, he begins to answer the question which the title
of the first chapter asks, adding epithet to epithet as
he attempts the impossible task of defining contemplation
in a way that will make it clear to all:

> Contemplation is the highest expression of man's
> intellectual and spiritual life. It is that life
> itself, fully awake, fully active, fully aware that
> it is alive. It is spiritual wonder. It is awe at
> the sacredness of life, of being. It is gratitude
> for life for awareness and for being. It is a
> vivid realization of the fact that life and being
> in us proceed from an invisible, transcendent and
> infinitely abundant Source. Contemplation is, above
> all, awareness of the reality of that Source. It
> knows the Source, obscurely, inexplicably, but with

a certitude that goes beyond reason and beyond simple
faith. For contemplation is a kind of spiritual
vision to which both reason and faith aspire, by
their very nature, because without it they must
always remain incomplete (V 14).

In contemplation, intellect and spirit aspire, through
reason and faith, to a kind of vision, a way of seeing,
characterized by awareness, by awe (in NSC, "spontaneous
aw," V 14) and by gratitude. Different phrases compete
in Merton's mind for the status of the ultimate definition of contemplation. It is a number of things: "the
highest expression of man's intellectual and spiritual
life"; "awe at the sacredness of life"; "awareness of
the reality" of the Source of life and being; "spiritual
wonder." These parallel definitions are evidence of the
impossibility of settling, even in the realm of positive
statement, on any one definition--which would thereby ex-
clude other equally applicable statements. He must therefore talk around the subject, admit by this plurality of
definition that contemplation escapes propositional con-
finement, and start to use the language of negation. The
passage above represents, in fact, the limit to which
(in a chapter on what contemplation is) Merton was able
to go before having to say what it is not.

Yet contemplation is not vision because it sees
"without seeing" and knows "without knowing". It
is a more profound depth of faith, a knowledge
too deep to be grasped in images, in words, or
even in clear concepts. It can be suggested by
words, by symbols, but in the very moment of trying
to indicate what it knows the contemplative mind
takes back what it has said, and denies what it has
affirmed (V 14).

"This" and "not-this," "so" and "not-so"--these are the
poles of necessary alternation between which Merton
moves in his description of contemplation. Only by a
union of these opposites, an end to their discrete duality, a recognition that one is dealing with a complexio
oppositorum which is at the same time a simplex intuitio
veritatis, can error be avoided. Even then, the experience is more positive than the positive expressions can
suggest, and, similarly, the negative expressions must
themselves be negated. We know, as he adds in NSC, not
so much by "unknowing" as by a reality "beyond all knowing or unknowing" (V 14--emphasis Merton's). If we do
not say this at some point, then unknowing (taking, after
all, the form of a gerund) becomes as much of a spiritual
commodity as contemplation is in danger of becoming. This
bipolar language cannot be integrated fully into any propositional statement or set of statements; it can only
be integrated in the contemplative person, the human
being as contemplative. The perspective of discussion,
on this understanding, then shifts to that of life as
lived by such a person. So we read that the contemplative
is one who reaches out "to the experience of the transcendent and inexpressible God" (V 15). He offers himself
to be "touched by God" (V 16), that is, "by Him Who has
no hands" (V 15), and to be "spoken" into existence by
"a call from Him Who has no voice" (V 16). She responds
to this God, answers and echoes God.

> Contemplation is this echo. It is a deep resonance[10]
> in the inmost center of our spirit in which our very
> life loses its separate voice and re-sounds with
> the majesty and the mercy of the Hidden and Living
> One (V 16).

It is derivative and contingent, this response of creature

to Creator, and so "re-sounds"; and it is connatural, a
testimony in human beings themselves to their capacity
for divinization, in that it "resounds."

> We ourselves become His echo and His answer. It is
> as if in creating us God asked a question, and in
> awakening us to contemplation He answered the ques-
> tion, so that the contemplative is at the same time
> question and answer (V 16).

> There is the flavor of Zen in this last quotation.
It suggests that in contemplation, the contemplative experiences herself or himself as both koan and its answer-
which-is-no-answer, but rather an intuition of being beyond any subject/object or question/answer duality. Yet
this use of the question/answer approach impels Merton
to deny that he is speaking philosophically, metaphysi-
cally, or in any way abstractly. Contemplation is "poor
in concepts, poorer still in reasoning" (V 18), and able
thereby to leave all and follow the Word in his divine
poverty (cf. 2 Corinthians 8.9). Once again there is the
strongest kind of autobiographical undertone here; for
Merton had experienced his own life as a question without
an answer until he discovered his contemplative vocation;
yet even that vocation, in all its "simplicity," was one
of constant discovery of new questions within the answer
once thought to be "final."

> It can be seen by what we have so far said that Mer-
ton is under no illusion that his writing about contemplation or our reading about it can accomplish anything
permanent. Only through experience, only through contemplating, can one test out this complex simplicity of concept and non-concept.

> One who does not actually know, in his own life, the

nature of this breakthrough and this awakening to
a new level of reality cannot help being misled by
most of the things that are said about it (V 18).
So Merton is not attempting to explain contemplation, in
spite of the fact that in the new preface he does speak
of adding "explanations" (V 9), and in spite of his inve-
terate tendency in that direction.[11] But he will hint,
suggest, point at or symbolize (one thinks here of his
Zen calligraphies) what he has experienced. This mention
of hinting or pointing suggests that a poetry of contemplation or a calligraphy of contemplation can more easily
be set forward than can an adequate philosophy or psycho-
logy of contemplation; for contemplation is no more to
be identified with "trance or ecstasy" or with "mystical
frenzy" (V 23) than with the conceptual categories already mentioned.(Perhaps the way ahead on this is for
someone to write a study of Merton as clown, even as a
holy fool of the West akin to his brothers in the Russian
tradition. For when the clown gestures, do we not all
understand?)

Having then recognized that contemplation must be
separated from these supports of intellect and spirit--
of which it is notwithstanding, as Merton earlier affirms, the "highest expression" (V 14)--the contemplative undergoes a "tragic anguish," "a kind of trial by
fire" (V 25), in which he is compelled "to examine, to
doubt and finally to reject all the prejudices and conventions that we have hitherto accepted as if they were
dogmas" (V 25). The contemplative must prepare himself
for a "mystical death that completely separates him
from created things" (V 339). The end of this is that
"even apparently holy conceptions are consumed along with
all the rest" (V 26), not only prejudices and conventions,

but also what the Church accepts and teaches as actual
dogmas.[12] Merton calls this experience, for the contemplative, "the anguish of realizing that he no longer knows
what God is" (V 26--emphasis Merton's): and how then can
the contemplative continue to speak of God at all? In
words, only by paradox. In life, by the fidelity of his
or her sharing in the intersubjective reality of contemplative union with God, "the 'Thou' before whom our inmost
'I' springs into awareness. He is the I Am before whom
with our own most personal and inalienable voice we echo
'I am'" (V 26).

(b) The Self

Merton's emphasis on locating contemplation in the
life of the one contemplating serves to link the preceding
discussion with a second major area of development in TS2,
the self. In SC Merton had used the categories of "true
self" and "false self," which he equates in TS2 (and NSC)
with the "person" and the "individual." In Merton's usage,
the "individual" cannot engage in contemplation. It is
only the "person," "the deep transcendent self" (V 19)
that awakens in contemplation. This "person" is the "true
inner self," "indestructible and immortal" (V 464). On
the other hand, the superficiality of her "individuality"
(V 19) will be revealed as such to the contemplative who
is struggling towards full personhood. For contemplation
"is precisely the awareness that this 'I' is really 'not
I' and the awakening of the unknown 'I' that is beyond
observation and reflection and is incapable of commenting
upon itself" (V 20).

In developing his Christian personalism in this
fashion, Merton is careful to point out that he is not

identifying the "false self" with the body and the "true self" with the soul; for he wishes to disinfect his spirituality and that of his readers from the anti-creational bias of which monastic writings have so often been transmitters. The body is God's temple (cf. 1 Corinthians 6.19) as much as the soul, which means that "His truth, His perfect reality, is enshrined there" (V 46).

> Soul and body together subsist in the reality of the hidden, inner person. If the two are separated from one another, there is no longer a person, there is no longer a living, subsisting reality made in the image and likeness of God (V 46, cf. 465).

To equate the soul, therefore, with the "true self," or the "whole self" (V 46), is to fall into angelism; to equate the body with the whole self is to fall into sensualism. Neither fall, however, can be blamed on either body or soul as such, but on the false self, the self organized in separation from and hostility to God (cf. the NT sarx, "the flesh"). Merton's language is inconsistent at this point, for he calls these errors "the fault of the person himself" (V 47). If he were being consistent here with his personalist language elsewhere in TS2 and NSC, he would here have said "false self" or "individual"; for the "person," elsewhere in the text, is a human being restored, or at least on the way to restoration, a human being in union with the Creator.

> There can be alienation between body and soul, however, as between true and false selves. If there is, it is a sign to the contemplative that he or she has not yet "entered into the fullness of contemplation" (V 464).

> As long as there is an "I" that is the definite subject of a contemplative experience, an "I" that is aware of itself and of its contemplation, an "I" that

can possess a certain "degree of spirituality," then
we have not yet passed over the Red Sea, we have not
yet "gone out of Egypt" (V 464).
This is because the idea of possession of a certain degree
of spiritual achievement can only attach itself to the
false self, who lives "in the realm of multiplicity, activity, incompleteness, striving and desire" (V 464). The
true self, on the other hand, "is not the kind of subject
that can amass experiences, reflect on them, reflect on
himself, for this 'I' is not the superficial and empirical
self that we know in our every day life" (V 464-65). On
this admission, the Merton who is writing this, and re-
cording his reflections on his contemplative experience,
is his "false self"--and what then are his reflections
worth? But Merton's strictures on the inadequacies of
language save him and us from this perverse logic. They
help us to see in his references to the "not yet" of contemplation a notion of progress (so long as we keep ourselves undefiled from any notion of "degrees") in the contemplative life, in which gradually the superficial self
is cast down, one's fragile individuality is surpassed,
and the person of God's design is raised up. In the life
of contemplation, as he says,

> we have to begin with what we actually are. We have
> to start from our alienated condition. We are prodi-
> gals in a distant country ... and we must seem to
> travel far in that region before we seem to reach
> our own land ... (V 466).

In this image of the Prodigal, as in all the biblical fi-
gures of exile and return, the contemplative sees herself
and her experience portrayed. To use the terms which Merton inherited from his Cistercian forbears, the contemp-

lative will not confuse Egypt, regio dissimilitudinis,
with the Promised Land, regio similitudinis, but will follow the way of contemplation to the restoration of the
similitudo, the likeness of the image of God in which all
human beings are made, and will so come to his "true
reality in the eyes of God" (V 467).

Yet, as human ego, the repository of individuality
is "respected by God and allowed to carry out the function
which our inner self can not yet assume on its own" (V 466,
cf. p. 39, above). Merton says that this external self,
in fact, is not so much evil as inchoate,

> and the fact that it is unsubstantial is not to be
> imputed to it as some kind of crime. It is afflicted
> with metaphysical poverty: but all that is poor de-
> serves mercy. So too our outward self: as long as
> it does not isolate itself in a lie, is blessed by
> the mercy and the love of Christ. Appearances are
> to be accepted for what they are. The accidents of
> a poor and transient existence have, nevertheless,
> an ineffable value. They can be transparent media
> in which we apprehend the presence of God in the
> world. It is possible to speak of the exterior
> self as a mask: to do so is not necessarily to re-
> prove it (V 486-87, cf. 54, 465).

Merton speaks here of the ego in much the same way that
Carl Jung speaks both of the "persona," or external self,
and of the "shadow," or inferior aspect of the psyche,
both of which are in need of the love of the self to
whom they pertain. In another parallel to Jungian thought,
in which the self is the archetype of God, active in and
from the collective unconscious, Merton describes the
outward self as a mask which "may well be a disguise not
only for that man's inner self but for God, wandering as

pilgrim and exile in his own creation" (V 487). The resonances of this statement in Christian theology and in
the religious literature of the world are vast and intri-
guing, and beyond our examination here. Yet simply to
make another link between Jung and Merton in relation to
this passage, we may say that God (like the early Merton,
himself an exile) can be said to "wander" in the unconscious of the human race, masked by each human being's
external self or persona/shadow, until with the fullness
of contemplation (Jung would speak of individuation) God
begins, as Merton says, "to live in me not only as my
Creator but as my other and true self" (V 68). A human
being, then, according to Merton, sets out on the way
of contemplation understood as the way to human wholeness (Jung's term again: cf. NT "salvation," to which
Merton devoted a new passage in TS2, V 62-63) for the
true self, the imago Dei restored to its similitudo in
redeemed humanity.[13]

(c) Humankind Divided

A third major area of development concerns Merton's
understanding of humanity, divided in itself, as that
division is manifested on the social plane. His personalist view, in its social dimension, is at the base of
his statements on war and peace, hatred and self-hatred,
and what he calls "the theology of the devil" (V 150).
Just as through contemplation the true self seeks out
and approaches wholeness, so through hatred, a diabolical
parody of contemplative union, the false self engages in
activities which tend towards the proximate splintering
and ultimate destruction of the human race, the end of
which is the confusion of God's purpose and the victory

of hell. This hatred is "the sign and expression of loneliness, of unworthiness, of insufficiency" (V 124); and to
the degree to which any of these negative realities are
found in the one hating, he or she becomes the object of
self-hatred--of which some human beings are conscious,
and punish themselves needlessly and endlessly, whereas
others are unconscious or less conscious of it, and so
"realize it in a different form by projecting it on to
others" (V 125). This latter is a "strong and happy hate"
(V 125), which ends nonetheless in the destruction of
the one hating. Before this point, however, the hating
self feels itself supported by a "justifying God, ...
an idol of war, an avenging and blood drinking spirit"
(V 125). This also is a projection, this time onto the
personality of God, of the hatred which fills such
people. Socially, of course, this projection is trans-
mitted from generation to generation through religious
teaching and experience which presents a God of this
kind to the individual, and to which the individual in
her or his generation makes a further negative contribution.

From such "gods" and their images we were in principle delivered, says Merton, by "a God Who delivered
Himself to the Cross and suffered the pathological cru-
elty of His own creatures out of pity for them" (V 125),
not out of any notion of their worthiness or unworthiness,[14] but out of his infinite and transcendent mercy.
Yet men and women continue to serve these false and finally unreal gods; and between the complacent hate of
the man blind to any unworthiness in himself, and the
"general, searing, nauseating hate" (V 126) of a woman
obsessed with her unworthiness, such people receive
their own reward. In the face of this dark and terrible

immensity, an unaided human effort to be "loving"--to de-
pend on what Merton calls "humanistic love" (V 127)--is
futile in the extreme. To attempt this, even, is to be
under the illusion "that we hate no one, that we are mer-
ciful, that we are kind by our very nature" (V 127), and
thereby once again to deceive ourselves. We have received
from God, it is true, the command to love:

> but what must necessarily come before in order to
> make the commandment bearable and comprehensible
> ... is a prior commandment, to believe. The root
> of Christian love is not the will to love, but
> the faith that one is loved. The faith that one is
> loved by God. That faith that one is loved by God
> although unworthy--or, rather, irrespective of
> one's worth! (V 126: emphasis Merton's).

This is both psychologically sound and spiritually un-
assailable. Not far beneath the surface of these words,
I would conjecture, lies the memory of Merton's lack of
certainty about his mother's love, and the long-lasting
effects of her death so early in Merton's life. Here
Merton offers as the basic remedy for hatred/self-hatred
the acceptance of prevenient and historic grace, available from God through the faith-community even to that
person who has not experienced it from his own family
in the course of his passage to chronological maturity.
The beautifully-articulated statement in which he develops
this theme is placed by Merton in the middle of Ch. 10
of NSC ("A Body of Broken Bones"), which in SC and SCR
is simply a collection of aphorisms loosely put together.
A comparison of the passage (V 124-27) with the portions
of the chapter preceding and following will provide clear
demonstration of Merton's growth in understanding and in

his power of expression on this subject in the years between SCR and TS2.

Two later passages (V 148-50, 155-57) interpret the
same theme in the chapter entitled "The Moral Theology
of the Devil." This "theology" shows itself in the lives
of those who are unconscious of their self-hatred, and
are as a result obsessed with the evil in their world.
These persons cannot understand that the Cross is "a
sign of mercy" (V 149).[15] To them it is rather the sign
of the triumph of legal justice, the symbol of God's pleasure in the death of his Son and the Son's desire to be
punished by the Father. But such "theology" is really
magic, an expression of the desire to manipulate God in
the service of one's own projections. When the magic
fails, as it must, disillusionment follows, and the active
haters are then

> ready for the Totalitarian Mass Movement that will
> pick us up on the rebound and make us happy with
> war, with the persecution of inferior races or of
> enemy classes, or generally speaking, with actively
> punishing someone who is different from ourselves
> (V 156).

In the absolutist viewpoint so engendered, and the rejec-
tion of any suggestion that "we might perhaps all be more
or less at fault" (V 157), we are ready to accept an exaggerated distance between right and wrong, attach ourselves
firmly to our own notion of right, and set about making
a disaster area of the peace and unity of the human race.
What happens then is described by Merton in a long new
passage (V 178-87) inserted into the chapter, only three
pages long in SC, entitled "The Root of War is Fear."
Here he sets forth an analysis of the dynamic of war,
beginning with "that hatred of ourselves which is too deep

and too powerful to be consciously faced" (V 178), a
hatred which is accounted for by our seeing "an equivalent
amount of evil in someone else" (V 179). The need to exor-
cize this hatred then causes us to create "a suitable enemy, a scapegoat in whom we have invested all the evil in
the world" (V 179); and in the end, as we try to deal with
this exaggerated evil, we find that "there is no outlet
left but violence" (V 179). In such a situation, human
efforts and good intentions become "the objects of contempt and of hatred" (V 180). Human beings, because they
have absolutized the rightness of their own political i-
deals, which "are perhaps to a great extent illusions and
fictions" (V 182), are unable to see "any good or any
practicability" (V 182) in the political ideals of their
enemies; and so a standstill of mistrust settles in as
the standard climate for political relations short of the
state of war to which it points, and into which it can,
by any number of possible provocations, be transformed.

Merton's only hope for a way out of this "inextri-
cable tangle of good and evil motives" (V 182) is an eschatological one, which distinguishes between that love
of enemies which the gospel requires of all Christians,
and what can only be called a naively humanistic trust.

If we can love the men we cannot trust (without
trusting them foolishly) and if we can to some extent share the burden of their sin by identifying
ourselves with them, then perhaps there is some
hope of a kind of peace on earth, based not on the
wisdom and the manipulations of men but on the
inscrutable mercy of God (V 185).

In such a situation, the Christian responds, in the first
instance, by praying for peace. Yet how, we may ask, does

such prayer function, if indeed it functions at all? True
prayer for peace, answers Merton, is prayer which is conscious of and rooted in the solidarity of all humanity in
sin--the corporate false self, the old Adam/Eve writ large;
and it is prayer which has also taken cognizance of the
relativity of all political institutions.

> When I pray for peace I pray God to pacify not only
> the Russians and the Chinese but above all my own
> nation and myself. When I pray for peace I pray to
> be protected not only from the Reds[16] but also from
> the folly and blindness of my own country. When I
> pray for peace, I pray not only that the enemies
> of my country may cease to want war, but above all
> that my own country will cease to do the things that
> make war inevitable (V 187).[17]

This statement, strongly anticipatory of the events of
the later sixties and early seventies, and now again so
ominously in the mid-eighties, represents a view of
prayer for peace which was at the time of writing strongly
ascendant, as news of atrocities committed in the Vietnamese war by the United States entered the American
consciousness to an unprecedented degree, chiefly through
the instrumentality of television. The daily televised
presentation of the American military enterprise in Viet-
nam combined with people's knowledge of the atrocities
of the other side to create a mental image of war, probably for the first time in history on the grand scale,
which was a psychological and spiritual correlate to the
view of prayer for peace which Merton offers to us here.[18]

War, then, is the final triumph of hatred, and the
final flourishing of division. It is the inevitable condition of human beings who coinhere in sin, and in alienation
from the source of their life and being. It is the anti-

thesis to the social end of contemplation in its eschatological aspect, which begins with love and faith and ends
in union; and the contemplative, eschatologically conscious of the judgement of God upon the entire race, will
find herself engaging in prayer for peace on the basis
of these perceptions. It is clear from the context of
the discussion in TS2, however, that Merton at the time he
was writing was frustrated by the lack of these perceptions
among Christians or in society at large. He is aware, he
says, that some will consider the statement on prayer for
peace quoted above to be "utterly sentimental" (V 187), or,
he might have added, unpatriotic; and he ends this long
new passage with the sad question, "But who on earth listens?" (V 187). Still, he knew before he died that many
more were listening than had listened when he wrote this,[19]
that those who had not bowed the knee to Baal (cf. 1 Kings
19.18) were beginning to speak up in considerable numbers.
But his deepest faith was placed, as the work as a whole
indicates, as indeed his life-direction indicates, not in
any who might listen "on earth," but in the God who both
listens and speaks, in word and in silence, to persons
of faith.

(d) Faith

In SC, Merton had called faith "the beginning of contemplation" (V 196), and had affirmed that a person
without a healthily-conceived and functioning faith could
never become a contemplative. Faith was not, he had said,
"an emotion, not a feeling," "not a blind sub-conscious
urge towards something vaguely supernatural," nor "an
elemental need in man's spirit," nor even a "feeling of
God's existence" (V 196). But it was, he said, "first

of all an intellectual assent" (V 197), through which the
believer accepts truth as revealed.

In TS2, Merton demonstrated that what he had earlier
written, although true as far as it went, was no longer
sufficient. As Padovano comments, Merton's view of faith
in SC

> restricts the equally important intuitive and emo-
> tional dimensions of faith. It diminishes the risk
> and courage of belief. It underscores the doctrinal
> component of faith and its institutional definition
> .... Obedience rather than inner conviction is the
> motivating force behind many of his statements, even
> though he accepts them at face value.[20]

By 1961, Merton had come to the same conclusion. Yet he
begins his development by elaborating his affirmation
of faith as assent. It is more, he says, than "an assent
of the mind" (V 201); it must also be an assent of the
will, which can then lead to a "communion of wills," for
in faith one does not simply assent to propositions
about God, but "to God Himself. One receives God" (V 201:
emphasis Merton's). To reduce faith to an assent to
statements about God is to forget the fact that "faith
is a communion with God's own light and truth" (V 201).
This forgotten, the path will lead, not to deep faith,
and so to contemplation, but to "anxious hair-splitting
arguments" (V 202), and thereby to hatred and division.
Like the contemplation to which it leads, however, faith
joins the believer to God beyond words and their nega-
tions, concepts and their opposites.

> The importance of the formulas is not that they are
> ends in themselves, but that they are means through
> which God communicates His truth to us. They must
> be kept clear. They must be clean windows, so that

they may not obscure and hinder the light that comes
to us. They must not falsify God's truth. Therefore
we must make every effort to believe the right formu-
las. But we must not be so obsessed with verbal cor-
rectness that we never go beyond the words to the
ineffable reality which they attempt to convey (V 202).
To the contemplative, faith is above all "the opening of
an inward eye, the eye of the heart" (V 202). Only by the
total and personal assent by which this eye is opened can
theoria, the seeing of the invisible, be arrived at.

Again, Merton's first statement on faith as submission (V 203-08) seemed to him by the time of TS2 to need
amplification. In SC he had affirmed that "the gift of
an interior light" was the result of a "simple act of submission" (V 207). In TS2, he wished to make it clear that
faith as submission could be overstressed so as to appear
to be the "whole essence of faith" (V 209). There was
a danger, if the assent of the will was directed to anything or anyone less than God, of faith's being reduced
to an equation with obedience, as Padovano recognizes.
This could lead, in Merton's view, to a "forced suppres-
sion of doubt rather than the opening of the eye of the
heart" (V 209). Faith as assent and faith as submission,
developed and humanized by Merton's increased stress on
the autonomy of the human person (see V 53-54), must
therefore be seen as aspects of faith as communion. On
this understanding, faith is not "just one moment of the
spiritual life" (V 211-12) in which, once for all, one
gives assent or makes submission. It is rather "that acceptance of God which is the very climate of all spiritual
living. It is the beginning of communion" (V 212).

From this communion comes "a dimension of simplicity

and depth" (V 212) in our apprehension of experience, a
depth which is the "incorporation of the unknown and of
the unconscious into our daily life" (V 212) as believers.
Little, in comparison, can be completely absorbed through
the faculty of understanding; but through faith "the unknown and the known together in a living whole" (V 213)
are integrated in a way which transcends the limitations
of the external/superficial self. Faith teaches us not
only truths about God, but truths about ourselves, especially "in so far as our unknown and undiscovered self
actually lives in God" (V 213). Such a vew of faith was
to Merton crucially important and too little understood.

> Faith is not just conformity, it is <u>life</u>. It em-
> braces all the realms of life, penetrating into
> the most mysterious and inacessible depths not
> only of our unknown spiritual being but even of
> God's own essence and love. Faith then is the only
> way of opening up the true depths of reality, even
> of our own reality. Until a man yields himself to
> God in the consent of total belief, he must inevi-
> tably remain a stranger to himself, an exile from
> himself, because he is excluded from the most mean-
> ingful depths of his own being; those which remain
> obscure and unknown because they are too simple
> and too deep to be attained by reason (V 213).

It was at the time of his baptism as an adult that he had
formally yielded himself to God "in the consent of total
belief"--and we recall the centrality in that experience
of his request for faith as divine gift.[21] The next permanently decisive step in his pilgrimage was his entrance
into Gethsemani. There, as he grew into the life of contemplation, he began to discover "the most meaningful
depths of his own being," from which he had excluded him-

self during his earlier adult years by his failure to
yield himself, abandon himself, into the faith-relation-
ship.

The passage on faith just quoted could almost have
been written by Jung as a description of the effects of
the process of individuation and the functioning of the
collective unconscious. Merton follows it with a psychic
geography which only partly, however, matches Jung's understanding. He describes the conscious mind as "exceeded
in all directions" by the unconscious which is "'beyond'
it, whether above or below" (V 214). However, the conscious
mind should not be ruled by the "below" of the unconscious
("our animal nature," V 214), but by its "above," by its
spiritual element. Jung, by contrast, would speak of the
ego as containing the executive function before individuation has been achieved, whereupon it yields this to the
self. On Merton's thesis, faith governs the animal nature
by love, subjects the reason to the spirit, and brings
the whole person into unity with "the 'unknown' that is
above him" (V 214). In this "superconscious realm of
mystery" is hidden "the summit of man's own spiritual
being" (V 214), where according to traditional ascetic
metaphor God dwells.

Merton declares the source of this spiritual geography to be the "traditional theology of the Greek Fathers"
(V 215), via their concepts of psyche, nous and pneuma
(roughly, "soul," "mind," and "spirit"). These were trans-
mitted through the Latin middle ages as anima, animus
and spiritus, and were domesticated into the Cistercian
tradition by William of St-Thierry.[22] Psyche/anima is
"the realm of instinct and of emotion, the realm of auto-
matism in which man functions as a psychophysical organ-

ism"; nous/animus is the "mind as a masculine principle,
the intelligence that ... guides our activity in the
light of prudence and of thought"; and pneuma/spiritus
is the highest principle, in which "both the others are
joined and transcend themselves in union with God" (V 215).
In pneuma/spiritus alone is the full stature of the person
to be found.

> But these three are not numerically distinct. They
> are one. And when they are perfectly ordered in
> unity, while retaining their own rightful qualities,
> then man is reconstituted in the image of the Holy
> Trinity (V 216).

There is an implied inferiority of the feminine in this
construct, a reflection of the social reality of the times
of its origin and transmission. Merton in his turn has
simply passed on the outline as he received it (not having
had up to this time any contact with Rosemary Ruether).[23]
Anima and animus as Jung uses them, however, are parallel
terms, for the contrasexual element in the psyche of the
male and female respectively; they are not hierarchically
ordered as in the patristic and mediaeval schemata.

It is then the function of faith to open to us this
"higher realm of unity" (V 216-17), to integrate known
and unknown, animal and spiritual, masculine and feminine,
conscious and unconscious. In this integrative role, in
which assent and submission are subsumed, faith makes it
possible for contemplation to begin, and for human beings
to appropriate the union which is the fullness of contemplation. In other words, there is no point in the life of
the spirit at which, according to Merton, faith can be
said to have completed its work, and may accordingly be
dispensed with. Only at the eschaton, when faith becomes
seeing, will this be the case. Faith must continue, even

through "pure emptiness, ... poverty, dereliction and
spiritual night" (V 293); and it is in fact in such a
situation, when the human spirit is stripped of all illusion and consolation, that faith is deepened and empowered.
For, as Merton states, faith

> must be deep enough to subsist when we are weak, when
> we are sick, when our self-confidence is gone, when
> our self-respect is gone. I do not mean that faith
> only functions when we are otherwise in a state of
> collapse. But true faith must be able to go on even
> when everything else is taken away from us (V 295).

Rooted in intellectual assent and volitional submission,
experienced in communion and tested by desolation, faith
is not only the beginning of contemplation, but the contemplative's sustenance as the channel of receptivity to
grace, until the End. It serves the contemplative as rod,
staff and Weltanschauung, and is the integrative factor
in his or her life-style, action and prayer.

*

With the drafting of TS2, Merton had moved his major
work of spirituality from the largely atomistic and absolutist piety of the first three versions to a piety which
was strongly social, psychologically rich and markedly
pluralist and tolerant, while still integral to its
Christian origins. With only one further revision, NSC,
the work would reach final form. The focus of the last version, as of the first, was contemplation; but it was contemplation as viewed and depicted by a contemplative whose
life had become so much deeper, so much simpler and yet
so much more complex, through his richly pastoral and in-

tellectual experiences in the fifties. With TS2 the preparatory stages are concluded, and the contemporary encheiridion is ready to be presented to the wide and varied readership for which it was intended.

CHAPTER 7

NSC: THE CONTEMPORARY ENCHEIRIDION

New Directions published New Seeds of Contemplation
on 30 January 1962,[1] the day before Merton's forty-seventh
birthday.[2] It contained one blank leaf, four leaves of
front matter, prefatory material on pp. ix-xv, another
blank leaf, the text itself on pp. 1-297, and three blank
leaves at the end. Measuring 21 by 14.5 cm, it was bound
in dark green cloth. In advance of publication, excerpts
were published in the Catholic Worker, Jubilee, Fellowship
and the Pax Bulletin.[3] Passages were also included in A
Thomas Merton Reader.[4]

It received seven recorded reviews, all brief: four
were British, two were American, and one was Irish.[5] Six
of the seven regarded it as basically a revision of SC
(only one was cognizant of the existence of SCR[6]), calling
it a book which had been "deepened and expanded,"[7] or a
best-seller that in simply growing older had developed "a
body of thought."[8] The seventh reviewer simply repeated
without elaboration Merton's statement from the preface
that it was "a completely new book."[9] No reviewer identified any categories of revision, however, nor pointed to
any particular shifts in thematic interest or treatment
by which the newness (if such there truly was) of New
Seeds could be distinguished. Generally speaking, the
reviewer response to NSC was very different from the response to SC. The reviews of SC were longer, had appeared
sooner after publication, and had in many cases appeared

in secular periodicals: The New York Times Book Review.
the New Republic and the Saturday Review (see p. 65, n. 6,
above). Those of NSC were brief (often combined with a
review of another book), appeared two years and more
after publication, and with the exception of the notice
in the Sewanee Review, appeared in Catholic periodicals
only--a considerable irony, if one realizes how much
more pluralist is NSC compared to SC.

Later critics, however, were ready to grant it a
larger place in their estimates of Merton's achievement
than these first reviewers. As early as 1969, Aldhelm
Cameron-Brown (now abbot of Prinknash, Gloucestershire)
referred to it as "one of the few works of this century
which really may deserve to become a 'spiritual classic'."[10]
Conrad Hoover moved this assessment from the subjunctive
into the indicative mood when he stated that NSC "is a
contemporary spiritual classic which will be read for
hundreds of years."[11] George Woodcock is much of the
same mind, and expands on his estimation accordingly.

> The one book on the mystical path that can be in-
> cluded among Merton's major works, and that has
> been called a "spiritual classic," succeeds pre-
> cisely because its strategy is one of masterly
> indirection. Its scope embraces not only the con-
> templative and his special vocation but also his
> relationship to the temporal and physical world
> in which he continues to exist at the same time
> as he exists in the timeless world of the spirit.
> This is New Seeds of Contemplation.[12]

Merton himself placed it among those of his own writings
that seemed most significant to him, the ones belonging
to his fourth period at Gethsemani.[13] In examining the
textual advances made in NSC over all the earlier ver-

sions (remembering of course that in their references to
New Seeds these critics are including the entire substance
of TS2), I will be supporting these estimations, and ex-
ploring the ways in which NSC keeps pace with and reflects
Merton's own contemplative epektasis.

NSC was translated into German and Portuguese in 1963;
into French and Spanish in 1964; into Italian in 1965;
and finally into Serbo-Croat (no date given).[14] In the
form either of SCR (see p. 96, above) or of NSC, therefore,
this work has carried Merton's thought into fourteen different languages, four of which, significantly, are Asian
tongues, and another five of which are among the numerically
smaller European languages. In terms of translation, then,
as well as in terms of other categories of evaluation, it
ranks with his autobiography and journals as among his
most widely-distributed and highly-regarded writings.[15]

Still in print and selling steadily, the paperback
edition from which the text used in the variorum was taken was published by New Directions in 1972,[16] and received one brief review.[17]

*

At some point between handing over the text of TS2
to the publisher and the actual publication of New Seeds,
Merton went over the entire body of the work, making, in
his usual fashion, additions, subtractions and alterations, the sum of which will be found in the fifth and
final column of the variorum. A survey of the omissions
in that column, omissions which in most cases simply
streamline an overlong passage or mute a strident note,
reveals little of theological interest which has not al-

ready been remarked upon in relation to some of the se-
quences of omission originating in one of the earlier versions. Thus there is no particular need to examine them
in detail, amounting as they do to fewer than two dozen
sentences in all (V 38-39, 55, 111, 128, 134, 140, 140-41,
166, 196, 251-52, 312). Nor is there anything of particular note in the two rewritten passages (V 67, 115-16).
However, the smaller emendations are as usual of specific
interest, as are the brief additions frequently found at
the end of a chapter (and elsewhere) which I am calling
"words of wisdom"; and so under these two heads we shall
consider the material unique to the final text.

(a) Smaller Emendations

These alterations I have brought together into two
loosely-related groupings. The first gathers those texts
which point in some way or other to the thrust towards
autonomy in the believer and the humanization of his contemplative life and experience which is a notable characteristic of (TS2 and) NSC; the second collects those e-
mendations which have some ecumenical or interfaith import.

(i) Autonomy and Humanization

Two separate groups of statements concern the autonomy of the believer and a move towards humanization which
is closely allied in spirit to it. In contrast to TS1,
SC and SCR, in which the emphasis is on submission (the
monk's submission to his superior being the paradigm),
NSC (as TS2) places a positive emphasis on the autonomy
and personal dignity of the believer as child of God.
A few examples will suffice; in all of them a stronger emphasis than in the earlier texts is placed on the human

power of decision, i.e., on free will, through which autonomy is exercised and increased (and may also of course
be abused). It should be noted, too, that this impulse
towards autonomy so noticeable in NSC now makes it possible for us to recognize the beginnings of this shift
in the earlier versions.

On the unity of God and believers:

> When we belong to God's love we own all things
> in Him and offer them all to Him in Christ His
> Son. For all things are ours and we are Christ's
> and Christ is God's (V 42, TS1 and SC).

> When we are united to God's love we own all
> things in Him ... (V 42, SCR).

> When we are one with God's love, we own all
> things in Him. They are ours to offer Him in
> Christ His Son. For all things belong to the
> sons of God and we are Christ's and Christ is
> God's (V 42, NSC).

On God's presence in the believer after the age of
discretion:

> From then on God's special presence in us de-
> pends entirely on our own preferences (V 69,
> SC).

> From then on God's special presence in us de-
> pends on our own preferences (V 69, SCR).

> From then on God's special presence corresponds
> to our own free decisions (V 69, NSC).

In other places, Merton uses the word "consent" (V 33, 69)
to strengthen this emphasis; and in another context (V 59)
speaks of himself as "my own mistake," rather than the
earlier "a mistake," and thereby takes responsibility for

his own alienation, at least in personal if not organic
terms.[18]

Under this heading, another set of changes in SCR
can now be seen as foreshadowing in that version this
stress on autonomy in NSC: they concern the unitive experience in contemplation.

> What happens is that the separate entity that was
> you suddenly disappears and nothing is left but a
> pure freedom indistinguishable from infinite Free-
> dom .... the subject of any divided or limited or
> creature experience has vanished (V 469-70, TS1 and
> SC).

> What happens is that the separate entity that is
> you apparently disappears and nothing seems to be
> left but a pure freedom indistinguishable from in-
> finite Freedom .... the subject of any divided or
> limited or creature experience seems to have van-
> ished (V 469-70, SCR).

Taken out of context, the language of TS1 and SC might
be thought pantheistic. In fact, the later language of
SCR (and NSC--cf. V 211) takes a position parallel to
that of William of St-Thierry, who in describing the
unitive experience says that the contemplative becomes,
not God, but "that which God is."[19] In all these examples we can observe Merton in the process of feeling
after and finding the words which will express in the
most balanced way a theology of "sonship" (Merton might
by now have been saying "filiality"[20]), of the autonomy
of the believer in relation to God's omnipotence. He
also omits two brief passages which seem to point in
the other direction--one which seems to deny to the believer any real part in his continuing growth (V 55), and

one which implies that peace can only be found in submission to a spiritual director (V 312). Their omission in
NSC affirms Merton's desire to present the human person
as autonomous under God in creation, and able to share
through decision in the work of co-creation.

Another group of alterations parallels this emphasis by bringing out the role of the senses, the emotions
and human creativity in a balanced life of contemplation.
The good soil of "liberty and desire" in which the seeds
of contemplation grow becomes in NSC the soil of "freedom, spontaneity and love" (V 27). The great contemplatives are said to have "loved" created things rather
than simply to have "noticed" them; and to this change
is added the assertion that the saints "loved everything
and everyone" (V 37)--either, one has to say, something
of an exaggeration as restated, or else an assertion de-
manding a thorough reassessment of who is or is not a
saint! "Customs, fashions, styles and attitudes" are
listed as better examples of the contingent order which
can involve us in stagnation and spiritual decay than
are "clothes, architecture, poems, places" (V 218), which
are thereby freed to become sacramental, potential vehi-
cles of spirit. The intoxication of spiritual joy is
said to belong to the "sensual" level rather than, too
sweepingly, to the "human" level; and an accusing finger
is pointed in NSC only at "crude emotion," and not as in
the earlier versions "emotion" as such (V 401). And now
that emotion is permitted to the contemplative (who remains, after all, a human being, and not an angelic one),
Merton in NSC is unwilling only to let exterior things
"disturb" him; in the earlier versions he had been unwilling even to let them "touch" him (V 252).

Another set of such changes affords some amusement; it concerns the natural effects of "spiritual exuberance" (V 402).

When it is all over you have no more profit than you might have got from a couple of glasses of wine or a good swim--and monks neither drink wine (in America) nor do they swim (V 402, SC; a misplaced comma after "wine" in TS1 has been removed).

When it is all over you have no more profit than you might have got from a couple of glasses of champagne or a good swim--and monks neither drink champagne nor do they swim (V 402, SCR).

When it is all over you have no more profit than you might have got from a couple of glasses of champagne or a good swim (V 402, NSC).

One concludes that between March and December 1949 the monks of Gethsemani began to drink wine (so that Merton had to use champagne to exemplify indulgence), and that between the end of 1949 and early 1961 they took up swimming. More seriously, it is probable that Merton simply recognized the ludicrous tone of the original statement, possibly through teasing from his European confrères, with whom he kept in close touch, and who would find it just as silly as would any North American skeptic. With all the other changes noted in this section, this last one testifies to Merton's self-acceptance, and thereby to his acceptance of others. Certainly the comment about how the saints loved everything and everyone echoes his account of his second great conversion, the experience at the corner of Fourth and Walnut.

(ii) The Wider Ecumenism

A second area of interest concerns statements or terms
from the earlier versions altered in NSC for, conjecturally,
ecumenical or interfaith reasons. We have already noted the
excision in SCR of the passage on the magisterium and the
sensual dreams of the Sufis (V 229--see pp. 99-101, above):
its omission may have represented, even so early, the broad-
ening of Merton's sensitivity to the negative resonances
of many expressions common among Roman Catholics in that
proto-ecumenical era. A number of these changes simply involve the replacement of a narrower with a wider term, or
with a phrase less redolent of romantic piety or ultramon-
tane usage. Thus for "Catholic" we now read "Christian"
(V 12), in the passage in the "Author's Note" in which he
expresses the hope that the book contains nothing new to
the tradition; and he is now apparently quite willing to
perplex orthodox theologians, or so one might infer from
his omission of the assertion to the contrary (V 12).
Again for "faculties" we now read "spirit" (V 69); for
"your Superiors" (in a passage on humility) simply "o-
thers" (V 154); and for the baroque phrase "complicity
with the Host before him on the altar" the more broadly
and truly Catholic "union with Christ as priest and as
offering in the Eucharistic sacrifice" (V 255-56). This
is echoed later in the same passage where in NSC he says
that the priest at the altar is identified with "the Sa-
viour" (V 256: British spelling Merton's) rather than,
more abstractly, "the Host" (V 256). Finally, a second
negative reference to oriental religion (emphasis mine)
is excised.

If, like the mystics of the orient, you succeed in
emptying your mind of every thought and every desire,

> you may indeed withdraw into the center of yourself
> and concentrate everything within you upon the ima-
> ginary point where your life springs out of God; yet
> you will not find God (V 63).

The impossibility of finding God through personally-willed
"emptying" (what elsewhere Merton calls "self-hypnosis"--
see V 106-07) is now seen as a possible temptation for anyone essaying the contemplative path, not just oriental
mystics; and the task of dialogical editing begun in SCR
has advanced another step in the direction of respect
for and fairness to other faiths. To this we may now link
a change in SC, not noticeable in that version on its
own, in which Merton altered his statement in TS1 that
Christ was crucified by "Pilate and the Jews" to "Pilate
and the Pharisees" (V 121).[21]

Another area of shift of ecumenical import is that
of Merton's mariological language. The shift had begun
in SCR. There Merton had said that what people say about
Mary "sometimes" tells us more about them than about her,
rather than "generally" telling us more (V 262). Her sanctity was said to be "hidden" rather than (with exaggerated
feeling) "unknowable" (V 262). Another change brings her
closer to her fellow-members of the body of Christ.

> And all our sanctity depends on her will, on her
> pleasure. The ones she desires to share the joy
> of her own poverty ... are the ones who become
> great saints in the sight of God (V 272, TS1 and SC:
> in SCR "great saints" becomes "the greatest saints").

> And all our sanctity depends on her maternal love.
> The ones she desires to share the joy of her own
> poverty ... are the ones who share her closeness to
> God (V 272, NSC).

Of this text in SC Emile Cailliet had written the only
negative part of an otherwise laudatory review;[22] the
change from "her will ... her pleasure" to "her maternal
love" may have been an eventual bow in his direction, or
at least in the direction of those Christians to whom
the earlier statements about Mary would have been offen-
sive. Beyond these changes (and see also pp. 86-87, above),
the new material in TS2 had presented Mary as herself a
believer, ancilla Domini (the handmaid of the Lord, cf.
Luke 1.38) as well as regina caeli (queen of heaven: see
V 268-71). Yet, when Merton applies to her such phrases
as "hope of the world" (V 274: it first occurs in SCR
and is retained in NSC), it is clear to the Christian reader who is not a Roman Catholic that the task of ecumenical
convergence is incomplete. Still, this is his last major
statement in print about Mary; and his subsequent silence
may have effected his final contribution to the ecumenical
synthesis which is still being worked out.[23] Most significant, perhaps, thinking particularly of Merton as art-
ist, is the disappearance of the hymn Memento Dei Genitrix
and the plate of Our Lady of Fontenay from their places
at the front of SC and SCR (V 3-4, 6), a place outside
the text proper, and her integration into the text as
believer in the believing community. This was of course
the same treatment as she was accorded by Vatican II,
when the original document on her role in the economy of
salvation, rather than being constituted a separate schema,
became the basis instead for a chapter included in Lumen
Gentium ("A Light to the Nations"), the constitution on
the Church.[24]

(b) <u>Words</u> <u>of</u> <u>Wisdom</u>

"For to one is given by the Spirit the word of wisdom
..." (1 Corinthians 12.8, KJV).

In the period (1956-65) when Merton was writing the
journal-entries finally edited and published as <u>Conjec-</u>
<u>tures</u> <u>of</u> <u>a</u> <u>Guilty</u> <u>Bystander</u>, a period into which the wri-
ting and publication of TS2/NSC also falls, he was inte-
resting himself deeply in the Eastern Christian tradition, and its "sophianic" teaching.[25] Bamberger links
his interest in sophianic spirituality to his reading of
Solovyev,[26] and Rowan Williams to his interest in Evdokimov.[27] In this tradition, <u>Hagia</u> <u>Sophia</u> or "Holy Wisdom"
(and with this name one thinks immediately of the great
church/mosque of Constantinople, itself at one time an
ikon of the Eastern Christian world) is an "invisible
fecundity, ... a meek namelessness, a hidden wholeness"
which is "at once my own being ... and the Gift of my
Creator's Thought and Art."[28] It is the "Diffuse Shining
of God"[29] which embraces all God's creatures with ten-
derness and light. It is in some sense a means of participation in the world of God's original intention, Para-
dise-Not-Yet-Lost, "the world as first formed by the
creative Wisdom of God, the world before the Fall."[30] It/
she is God as Spirit, "God Himself as Gift"[31] (there seems
to be no easy resolution to the inconsistency of gender-
related pronouns in Merton's discussion of this subject).

Merton's interest in the sophianic tradition, which
I see as the correlate for what I will be characterizing
in this chapter as the "words of wisdom" in NSC, shows
up in a number of places in <u>Conjectures</u>. In one passage
he presents wisdom as a facility for "the recapitulation
of culture and civilization in Christ"[32] in the wise person; and he sees his own vocation very much in these terms,

as does Bertrand de Margerie, who calls him "one of the
wise men of the Kingdom."[33]

> ... I am more and more convinced that my job is to
> clarify something of the tradition that lives in me,
> and in which I live: the tradition of wisdom and
> spirit that is found not only in Western Christendom
> but in Orthodoxy, and also, at least analogously,
> in Asia and in Islam. Man's sanity and balance and
> peace depend, I think, on his keeping alive a con-
> tinuous sense of what has been valid in his past.[34]

Later he says that he prays to have a wise heart, and
describes the attraction which Julian of Norwich has for
him in terms which suggest how his own vocation was ripe-
ning.

> She is a true theologian with greater clarity, depth
> and order than St. Theresa .... She first experienced,
> then thought, and the thoughtful deepening of ex-
> perience worked it back into her life, deeper and
> deeper, until her whole life ... was simply a matter
> of getting saturated in the light she had received.[35]

We see this same dynamic in the whole process of maturation which for Merton leads from TS1 to NSC: experience,
thought, and the "thoughtful deepening of experience"
which we have seen in Merton's reworking of basic themes.
He was actively and synthetically clarifying the tradition that lived within him, and in which he lived and
prayed. For Julian, the heart of theology was a remaining
in the midst of life's contradictions, but in peace,
knowing deeply that "all manner of thing shall be well,"
even though God's resolution of the contradictions of
history remain secret to many, even to most.

To have a "wise heart," it seems to me, is to live

> centered on this dynamism and this secret hope--
> this hoped-for secret. ... the "wise heart" remains
> in hope and in contradiction, in sorrow and in joy,
> fixed on the secret and the "great deed" which
> alone gives Chrisian life its true scope and dimen-
> sions![36]

By living in this way, Merton suggests in dozens of contexts, he has been able to take the experiences of his
life before and after he arrived at Gethsemani, to identify the spiritual possibilities which even their contradictions contain ("I have become convinced that the very
contradictions in my life are in some ways signs of God's
mercy to me"[37]), and by recapitulating in writing his
sense of how his experiences and the great tradition inter-
sect, to share these possibilities with others.

> ... I work my life into another dimension in which
> these things ... become less and less _my_ experien-
> ces. They are more and more woven into the great
> pattern of the whole experience of man, and even
> something quite beyond all experience. I am less
> and less aware of myself simply as this individual
> who is a monk and a writer, and who, as monk and
> writer, sees this, or writes that. It is my task
> to see and speak for many, even when I seem to be
> speaking only for myself.[38]

Here it seems that when he refers to "another dimension"
he is referring to wisdom in sophianic perspective. It
is by this wisdom, wisdom from God, that his human possibilities and experiences are being taken up into
"something quite beyond all experience," that is, into
contemplation. Inseparable from this is his consciousness of his vocation as a representative one, a vocation to see and to speak for many, a vocation to be the

"holy man of our time" (in John S. Dunne's phrase). Hinson
makes the same point.

> The somewhat surprising reception his writings re-
> ceived in the secular world made him and his super-
> iors realize that it was not monks alone who sought
> and needed the contemplative message. Consequently,
> in writing for monks he saw that he was also writing
> for others.[39]

We have already quoted Hinson's estimation of Merton's
uniqueness as one who had recapitulated the entire western Christian tradition in himself (p. 7, above); and in
these intuitions of himself as sage, as man of wisdom,
we find Merton confirming this.

But wisdom, even humanly considered, is more than
cultural recapitulation or chronological maturation: it
is also that power of God and in God by which the contemplative is herself grasped. Merton here describes wisdom in such a way that we know him to be referring to
contemplation and to his own experience of it.

> ... he who is truly wise is seized by wisdom. He
> does not gain possession of wisdom by his own
> power--or by any other. To be wise, is, in a
> sense, to abandon every attempt at gaining wis-
> dom, and to enter into a whole new dimension of
> existence, where the division of subject and
> object, ends and means, time and eternity, body
> and soul either appears in a totally new perspec-
> tive or vanishes altogether. ... From such unified
> existence come the aphorisms of great Asian con-
> templatives or Christian saints--and the poems
> of Zen masters.[40]

This description by Merton of how wisdom in the wise

person issues forth in aphoristic or poetic statement is directly applicable to the "words of wisdom" which comprise virtually the entire body of the specifically new material in NSC. There are some score of these in the text proper, to which we may add the Latin epigraph (V 6) which may have been the replacement in NSC of the Latin hymn in SC and SCR (V 3-4).

Typically, a word of wisdom comes at the end of a discussion of some subject, and conveys a note of maturity, finality and (sometimes) tranquillity; seven of them are in fact the concluding word of particular chapters in NSC (V 190, 324-25, 343-44, 364-65, 380, 397-98, 406). One can almost visualize Merton reading the proofs of NSC, and with no little satisfaction adding these brief, sage codicils. That he ends six of them (V 85, 94, 134-35, 189, 324-25, 418) with an exclamation mark is stylistic evidence for this speculation.

Their subject-matter is as varied as the contexts in which they occur: liberty (V 364-65), detachment (343-44), distractions (V 364-65), the person entering Paradise (V 374), or the gift of understanding (V 380). A number of them seem to be distillations of his personal experience: his resolution of his view of himself as saint and/or sinner (V 94); his dismissal of the "problem" of the love of other persons as an obstacle to contmplation (V 110); his attempt to deal with his own projections (V 190). They are often bearers of encouragement, a word from one who has passed successfully through the fires (V 364-65), 397-98). Two examples may be cited: the first refers to the gift of sainthood, the second to solitude.

It teaches them to bring the good out of others by compassion, mercy and pardon. A man becomes a saint

not by conviction that he is better than sinners but
by the realization that is one of them, and that all
together need the mercy of God! (V 94: cf. the
Fourth and Walnut experience).

How can people act and speak as if solitude were a
matter of no importance in the interior life? Only
those who have never experienced real solitude can
glibly declare that it "makes no difference" and
that only solitude of the heart really matters!
One solitude must lead to the other! (V 134-35: cf.
his long struggle for the hermitage).

This last one is not noticeably tranquil; but in general,
they are calm, summary expressions of one in whom the
"invisible fecundity" of God's wisdom has been fruitfully
at work. By faith (V 216), he has entered a

higher realm of unity, of strength, of light, of
sophianic love, where there is no longer the
limited and fragmentary light provided by rational
principles, but where the Truth is One and Undi-
vided and takes all to itself in the wholeness of
Sapientia or Sophia (V 216-17).

The sophianic person is not limited simply to thought,
to "mere 'mentality'" (V 216), that is, to ratiocination;
nor is he the creature of "a purely emotional worship"
(V 216). Anyone who is limited to either of these poles
must be said, in fact, to be living a seriously incomplete life. Rather, says Merton, to live sapientially
is to live in union and wholeness.

The true spiritual life is a life neither of dion-
ysian orgy nor of apollonian clarity: it transcends
both. It is a life of wisdom, a life of sophianic

love. In <u>Sophia</u>, the highest wisdom-principle, all
the greatness and majesty of the unknown that is in
God and all that is rich and maternal in His creation are united inseparably (V 216).

In sophianic love the contemplative transcends the
dualities of earthly existence and experiences the joy
of Paradise regained (V 374, 380; cf. 389). He has
passed beyond the "divisions"[41] caused by the Fall, and
he is on his way to realizing in his own personhood the
victory of Christ. It is this spiritual reality which
is so strongly communicated by the words of wisdom
which adorn the final text of NSC. With their addition,
the long work of editing and re-editing, refining and
balancing, is complete; and we have in our hands the
contemporary encheiridion.

                                      *

More than any other work of Merton's, <u>New Seeds of
Contemplation</u> does deserve this epithet of encheiridion.
It <u>is</u> comprehensive enough to be a spiritual handbook
for the serious and intelligent Christian of our day,
monastic or otherwise. It is the kind of book to which
one profitably returns again and again. It is wide-
ranging, covering everything from creation to recreation,
from sexuality to television, from war to solitude. It
has been worked upon and worked through, again and
again, in a way parallel to the process which Merton
had noted in Julian of Norwich, by means of which an
ever-deepening distillation of contemplative experience[42]
is clarified and re-presented. Unlike any of the older
encheiridia, however, it can speak directly to the
believer who deeply desires <u>both</u> to remain in touch with

"what has been valid"[43] in the Christian past, and who
is also struggling to work out the dimensions of his or her
contemplative vocation in the present world of potential
nuclear holocaust (cf. V 177-90), which of course threatens the continued transmission of our spiritual tradition
as it threatens every other aspect of human civilization.

Having dispensed with so many of the immaturities
of the earlier versions, yet having retained, clarified
and deepened what they contained of continuing value,
Merton in NSC brought his contemplative thought to its
highest point within the confines of one book. Flawed
and idiosyncratic as in some small respects it remains,
it is an outstanding gift from a wise and holy man to
the women and men of his own troubled generation in
particular, and as such a vital resource for those engaged in the spiritual searching of our time.

CHAPTER 8

THE RECOVERY OF PARADISE

The key word for Merton's thought, already mentioned
above, is <u>contemplation</u>. But there is also a key motif,
or complex of metaphors, through which Merton relates
his spirituality of contemplation to the scriptural revelation, thereby to the entire Christian community, and
through the Church to the generality of the human race.
(This is not to say that the Church at present understands its vocation in this way, but simply to say that
Merton sees at least part of the mission of the Church
to be a contemplative self-opening to the rest of human-
kind.) This key motif is <u>the</u> <u>recovery</u> <u>of</u> <u>Paradise</u>. In
the Bible it has three main sources: the exodus of the
Israelites from slavery in Egypt through testing in the
wilderness to their new home in the Promised Land (see
Exodus, Deuteronomy, Joshua); the exile of God's people
in Babylon, their languishing there as strangers in a
strange land, and their eventual return to Jerusalem
(2 Kings 25; Isaiah 35, 40.1-11, 48.12-22, 51.3; Ezekiel
36.33-36; Joel 2.3); and, most primally, the story of
the fall of humankind into the "region of unlikeness"
to God's image, with its consequences in the redemption
accomplished by Christ and in our human longing to appropriate that victory and so return to the "region of likeness" to God after whose image we were created (Genesis 3;
1 Corinthians 15.20-28, 42-49; Colossians 1.15-23). Merton summarizes this biblical message of liberation by

relating it to the contemplative's

> vocation to recover the paradise life after suffering
> temptation with Christ in desert solitude ... a
> variant of the fundamental themes of all Biblical
> theology: the pascha Christi, the call of the People
> of God out of Egypt, through the Red Sea into the
> Desert and to the Promised Land; the theme of the
> Cross and Resurrection, dying to sin and rising in
> Christ; the theme of the old and new man; the theme
> of the fallen world and the new creation.[1]

As a man on a journey, a man in exile from himself in
various contemporary Babylons, and a man conscious of
himself as fallen, Merton was strongly attracted, on many
levels, to the prospect of recovering Paradise. From his
reading of Dante at Cambridge, a study which eventually
covered at least the years 1933-41, on and off, he had
encountered the notion of the Earthly Paradise, in which
Adam and Eve, had they not fallen, would have lived with
their descendants until God's time for them to be directly
assumed into heaven.[2] He subsequently identified this
Earthly Paradise with monastic life, specifically with
the life lived at the abbey of Gethsemani.

> Abbeys are paradises, in two different senses. That
> they are at the same time earthly (material) and
> spiritual (heavenly) paradises is the fruit of a
> paradox. They are both only because they are pur-
> gatories. ... This abbey ... is an excellently well-
> ordered kind of society .... at the same time a
> holy place and one of the best communities, or so-
> cieties in the earthly sense, in the country ....[3]

The paradisus claustralis, Merton seems to be saying,
must be recognized as both earthly and heavenly if its

full significance is to be perceived. As a well-ordered
society in a chaotic world, it is an earthly paradise;
and as "holy place," ordered (as is heaven) around the
worship of God, it is a heavenly paradise. For Merton
this sense of the paradisaical quality of Gethsemani
was constellated out of many factors: his rootless early
life and the comparatively early loss of his parents;
the chaos of contemporary western society; his romantic
and poetic temperament; and his nostalgia for the world
of the middle ages, conceived out of his family situation, born on his European travels, nourished by his studies at Cambridge and Columbia, and now suddenly acces-
sible in the countryside of Kentucky.[4]

Having thus recovered Paradise on the geographical
and vocational level, Merton then set himself at Gethsemani to the exploration of monastic history and spirituality in all its breadth. Here he encountered the connection made by Gregory of Nyssa, Gregory the Great and
others between the life of contemplation and the return
in spirit to the Eden of God's original intention for
the human race.[5] In this tradition, Paradise is once
again earthly, but earthly by experience rather than by
geographical discovery; it is the summit of human capa-
bility, at which a human being "experiences to some extent a restoration to the spiritual condition of Adam"[6]--
before the fall, that is. The "lower levels" (V 339, TS2)
of contemplative prayer constitute the ladder by which
one climbs back up the mountain of Purgatory "to a restoration of the lost grace of Paradise and to the vision
of God."[7] In the Cistercian tradition, this process was
commonly described as the journey from the "region of
unlikeness" (Egypt, Babylon, sin) to the "region of likeness" (Canaan, Jerusalem, redemption).[8] According to this

view, the human person, made in God's image, has lost,
not the image itself, but its <u>similitudo</u>, the likeness
of the image to Christ, its original, through sin deriv-
ing from the fall, and will only regain it when he or she
returns to God in perfect love.[9]

Merton's fullest statement in one place of the motif
of the recovery of Paradise is found in an article of the
same name, first published in 1961, the same year in
which he was preparing the publication of <u>New Seeds</u>.[10]
In this article he reasserts the patristic tradition that
the Paradise of monastic seeking is an earthly and not
a heavenly state, that it "belongs more properly to the
present than to the future life."[11] But although in a
very real sense "earthly," it was neither geographical
nor material. Rather,

> what the Desert Fathers sought when they believed
> they could find "paradise" in the desert, was the
> lost innocence, the emptiness and purity of heart
> which had belonged to Adam and Eve in Eden. ...
> They sought paradise in the recovery of that "unity"
> which had been shattered by the "knowledge of good
> and evil."[12]

In Adam and Eve, this human unity had been shattered by
their fall away from wisdom/<u>Sophia</u>/<u>sapientia</u>, from loving
union with God; in Christ, New Adam, human unity with
God, had been in principle and <u>in potentia</u> restored. In
him all persons now had the opportunity to return to
God's intention for humankind, in innocence and purity.
As mentioned in the last chapter, this is the goal of
sophianic spirituality, the overcoming of the "divisions"
caused by the fall, divisions which

> are transcended in the first place by the Incarna-

tion, and it is for each man in Christ to realise
this victory in his own existence and so partake
in the total restoration of the cosmos.[13]

The contemplative will thus try to take into his or her
own life the victory of Christ as fully as possible, recover Eden by making its recovery the heart's desire,[14]
and devote himself/herself heart and soul to the quest
for "the purity of original innocence."[15]

Here a problem arises, however, the tension between
"innocence" and "knowledge"--between Sophia/sapientia
and gnosis/scientia. By "knowledge," Merton means ratiocination and the trust in one's own ratiocinative power
as the characteristic and hyperautonomous act of human
consciousness estranged from God, mythically represented
in the story of the eating of the fruit of the tree of
the knowledge of good and evil (Genesis 2.17, 3.1-7).

> The knowledge of good and evil ... makes the soul
> conscious of itself, and centers it on its own
> pleasure. It becomes aware of what is good and evil
> "for itself." As soon as this takes place, there
> is a complete change of perspective, and from unity
> or wisdom ... the soul now enters into a state of
> dualism. It is now aware of both itself and God,
> as separated beings. It now sees God as an object
> of desire or fear, and it is no longer lost in Him
> as in a transcendent subject.[16]

In Lévy-Bruhl's term, participation mystique is no more,
and the sometime participator in the mystical unconscious
has been plunged into the icy waters of self-consciousness.
This shattering of transcendent unity is the chief effect,
in the vertical dimension, of the fall, and accounts for
the origin of the false self, "the disfigured image, the
caricature, the emptiness that has swelled up and become

full of itself, so as to create a kind of fictional sub-
stantiality for itself."[17] Thus when the true self,
through contemplation, has regained "innocence," regained Paradise, then "knowledge" as its chief mode of
the appropriation of reality will, as St Paul says, "vanish away" (1 Corinthians 13.8, KJV). In the meantime,
however, as Merton says, "it is a question of treating
knowledge and innocence as complementary realities."[18]
The Desert Fathers in a number of instances wanted to
abandon knowledge altogether as they sought innocence.
But they also realized that a person can reach a state
of pure "unknowing" in which he recognizes himself to be
"a master of spiritual knowledge"[19]--hence Merton's brief
comment, added in NSC, that "we know beyond all knowing
or 'unknowing'" (V 14). For paradoxically, the master
of unknowing exercises his mastery in the realm of sci-
entia, the "realm where man is subject to the influence
of the devil,"[20] to temptation and corruption. True purity of heart, however, as distinct from this penultimate
but finally insufficient mastery of impurity, comes only
with the long exercise of spiritual discretion[21] that
leads to quies--freedom in contemplation from all images
and concepts, with the reaching of which the contemplative is living once more in innocence, and "is now fully
his true self because he is lost in God."[22] Yet he would
never have reached it without the knowledge of its desi-
rability and attainability; nor would he have reached it
if he had rested in any form of that knowledge, even the
highest, even the knowledge of unknowing.

But even the realized state of contemplation is not
the ultimate stage on the paradisaical quest. Innocence
is indeed the recovery of Paradise. But because Paradise

is not heaven, its recovery is

> in fact, only a return to the true beginning. It is
> a "fresh start." The monk who has realized in him-
> self purity of heart, and has been restored, in
> some measure, to the innocence lost by Adam, has
> still not ended his journey. He is only ready to
> begin. ... Purity of heart ... is the intermediate
> end of the spiritual life. But the ultimate end is
> the Kingdom of God.[23]

It might be said that when a person then engages in the
ongoing struggle for the Kingdom, that person has returned
to the realm of the dualities, and there is thus no permanent point to the quest for innocence: one has again
been cast out of Eden. But according to Merton this is
not the case. The first and human struggle for the recovery of Paradise, is indeed to some extent a struggle
between good and evil, or between better and best, but
it is a struggle on the individual/personal level. The
second and eschatological struggle, the struggle for the
Kingdom, is the contemplative's participation not simply
in the human struggle, but in

> the work of the <u>new creation</u>, the resurrection from
> the dead, the restoration of all things in Christ.
> ... The world was created without man, but the new
> creation which is the true Kingdom of God is to be
> the work of God in and through man. It is to be
> the great, mysterious, theandric work of the Mys-
> tical Christ, the New Adam, in whom all men as
> "one Person" or one "Son of God" will transfigure
> the cosmos and offer it resplendent to the Father.[24]

Here again, even with such exalted referents, we are (as
Merton points out) once again in the realm of knowledge;
but now it is a knowledge that <u>serves</u> innocence rather

than competing with it or preventing its realization.

It is a dynamic epitomized by this relation of knowledge and innocence which is, it seems to me, the critical
dynamic of TS2/NSC, and perhaps the inner current which
distinguishes it most clearly from the earlier versions
of 1948-49. In its simplest terms, it represents a balancing of the scholasticism dominant in the earlier versions with the influence of Zen in the later, the balancing of reasoning with intuition (see n. 18, above).
It will be remembered what a tremendous respect for Catholic philosophy Merton gained from Gilson's Spirit of
Mediaeval Philosophy, especially through his discovery
in its pages of the notion of aseitas.[25] This new attitude on his part was nourished by his studies with Dan
Walsh, and by the dominance of Thomism in the theology
which he learned in the novitiate.[26] Yet even in this
early period, Walsh had suggested to him that his bent
was not so much scholastic as Augustinian, or as Merton
summarizes it,

> not so much towards the intellectual, dialectical,
> speculative character of Thomism, as towards the
> spiritual, mystical, voluntaristic and practical
> way of St. Augustine and his followers.[27]

Hinson believes that this was an accurate assessment,
and on its basis maps out the course of Merton's developing attitude to scholasticism.

> Somewhere along the line ... scholastic interests
> decreased as mystical interests increased. ...
> Indeed, there is early evidence to show that he
> chafed and groaned with a scholastic yoke. In
> his journal entry of August 4, 1949, he expressed
> a desire to possess more of the Dominican traits of

> "sharpness, definiteness, precision in theology,"[28]
> but he did not own them. Later on, in <u>Conjectures</u> of
> <u>a</u> <u>Guilty</u> <u>Bystander</u>, he wrote more critically. ...
> Finally, according to second-hand information, in
> his last years Merton would walk away from discus-
> sions of scholasticism. It ran too much against the
> grain for one who sought the intuitive apprehension
> of reality.[29]

However, it should be emphasized that Merton had no problems with St Thomas himself, whose "spirit and perspectives"--awareness of the world of his time, interest in
reason and scripture, and openness to the non-Christian
culture of Aristotle and Islam[30]--remained intensely re-
levant, as far as Merton was concerned. His problem was
rather with those Thomists (Dan Walsh certainly not among
them[31]) who in clear contradiction of the "spirit and
perspectives" of St Thomas, had "closed him in upon himself in a little triumphalist universe of airtight cor-
rectness," and had thereby "unconsciously sealed off his
thought in such a way that in order to embrace Thomism
one has to renounce everything else."[32]

But in the mid-to-late fifties, the period just
preceding the writing of TS2 and the publication of NSC,
Merton (as many have recognized) was coming under the
influence of Zen. No longer satisfied with scholasticism's
analytic character, he found himself attracted to the
meta-synthetic and intuitive perspectives of Zen, to its
delicacy and grace, and to the opportunities that it
gave him to encounter Asian contemplatives and traditions.[33] Zen was not a religion, not a theology, not an
ethical system per se, not a philosophy in the discursive
or analytic sense; it therefore presented no threat to
the integrity of his membership in the Roman Catholic

Church nor to his inner consciousness of himself as a
Christian. But it <u>could</u> be described by all the terms
which Merton had used of himself in response to Dan Walsh's
intuition about the bent of his temperament: it was spiritual, mystical, voluntaristic and practical. It was, paradoxically, Merton's Augustinianism that reached out to
the Asian wisdom of Zen, balancing in a wonderful way the
fact that it was an Asian monk, Bramachari, who had first
suggested to Merton that he read Augustine.[34] Zen, as the
way to the <u>simplex</u> <u>intuitio</u>, to <u>satori</u>, to the resolution
of all dualities, appealed to a mind that had originally
benefited from and then been exhausted by the analytic
approaches of scholasticism.[35] Merton at this point in his
life was looking for synthesis, not analysis; for mystical
union in depth rather than intellectual or apologetic rein-
forcement for his faith. According to Woodcock, Merton's
apprehension of Zen was unusually good for a westerner, a
non-Zennist by background; and he quotes Suzuki as having
remarked that Merton "grasped it with a sharper intuition
than any other western student"[36] of his acquaintance.

These considerations granted, we are now in a position
to trace something more of the critical dynamic of the text
of TS2 and NSC. Once again it should be affirmed that there
is no question of knowledge being forgotten, or obliterated
by innocence, of reason being replaced by intuition, of
scholasticism being ousted by Zen.[37] It is rather a balancing, a move towards wholeness as over against the hyper-
rational, dry onesidedness of Merton's earliest theological
formation. We have already connected this search of Merton
for wholeness to the sophianic spirituality which was engaging him during the same period. It also shows up strong:
in his strictures on Descartes, in a disinclination which

went back as far as the time of writing of the <u>Mountain</u>.
Thus in Ch. 2 of the new material in TS2 he writes:

Nothing could be more alien to contemplation than
the <u>cogito</u> <u>ergo</u> <u>sum</u> [I think, therefore I am] of
Descartes. ... This is the declaration of an alien-
ated being, in exile from his own spiritual depths,
compelled to seek some comfort in a <u>proof</u> <u>for</u> <u>his</u>
<u>own</u> <u>existence</u> (!) based on the observation that he
"thinks." ... He is reducing himself to a concept
.... At the same time, by also reducing God to a
concept, he makes it impossible for himself to
have any intuition of the divine reality which is
inexpressible (V 20-21).

Contemplation, on the other hand,

is the experiential grasp of reality as <u>subjective</u>
.... Contemplation does not arrive at reality after
a process of deduction, but by an intuitive awakening in which our free and personal reality becomes
fully alive to its own existential depths, <u>which</u>
<u>open</u> <u>out</u> <u>into</u> <u>the</u> <u>mystery</u> <u>of</u> <u>God</u> (V 21).

In taking this approach, Merton was reacting against a
Cartesianism which "placed conceptualization before
being."[38] In the centuries since Descartes, moreover,
this tendency to hyperconceptualization had resulted in
a widespread tendency to objectify the self, the very
ground of subjectivity. In <u>Conjectures</u> Merton makes a
general comment on this process, a comment which indubi-
tably represents an experiential view.

The taste for Zen in the West is in part a healthy
reaction of people exasperated with the heritage of
four centuries of Cartesianism: the reification of
concepts, idolization of the reflexive consciousness, flight from being into verbalism, mathematics

and rationalization. Descartes made a fetish out of
the mirror in which the self finds itself. Zen shat-
ters it.[39]

Two small but significant alterations in NSC reinforce
this view. In TS2, Merton had said that contemplation, as
something beyond art and philosophy, was also "beyond theology": in NSC, he alters this to "beyond speculative theology" (V 14), to make it clear that he is not talking
about theologia--in the language of Evagrius, the highest
contemplation.[40] Then at the end of Ch. 20 ("Tradition and
Revolution"), in concluding a discussion on how the contemplative is to convey to others the meaning of contemplation,
he had in the earlier version said this: "beware of the
contemplative who says that scholastic theology is all
straw [St Thomas' comment, at the end of his life] before
he has ever bothered to read or understand any" (V 235,
TS1--"or understand" was omitted in SC). Then in NSC he
omitted the word "scholastic." Theology as such of course
remains; but Merton is making clear that for him, scholastic theology is no longer the norm of theological reflection.

In other contexts in TS2/NSC, Merton gives added
stress to the attainment of paradisaical innocence (V 36-37,
338-39, 374, 380, 389). The notion had been there in germ
as early as TS1 (V 112, 374, 379), but it had been over-
shadowed by the dominating presence of scholasticism, by
an emphasis, in other words, on knowledge. In NSC, however,
a new framework for the entire book was provided by the
completely new material of Chs. 1 and 2 (which as we have
already seen discuss the problematic of contemplation in
terms of Merton's post-scholastic and anti-Cartesian point
of view), and by Ch. 39 ("The General Dance"), which draws

together and universalizes the themes of the book as a
whole. Merton's purpose in these chapters, epitomized by
the motif of the recovery of Paradise, is to rescue contemplation from the elitist fate which it has often suffered at the hands of gnosticizers--those restricted to
a reliance on "knowledge" alone without innocence--and
to restore it to the generality of the Church, and through
the Church (Israel as servant of the nations: cf. Isaiah
2.1-5) to the generality of the human race.

For the recovery of Paradise, although very much a
Christian and monastic notion, ultimately refers neither
to a Christian nor to a monastic constituency alone, but
to humankind in its entirety, to all the heirs of the
first humans in the Jewish and Christian myth of Adam and
Eve. As Merton says in a later work, the contemplative
is conscious by virtue of his vocation that he lives in
an age of deep searching and struggle, even of revolution;
and his vocation requires him, not to cut himself off
from the world, but to love the world by fidelity to his
contemplative calling. In fact, he

> abandons the world only in order to listen more in-
> tently to the deepest and most neglected voices
> that proceed from its inner depth. This is why the
> term "contemplation" is both insufficient and am-
> biguous when it is applied to the highest forms
> of Christian prayer. Nothing is more foreign to
> authentic monastic and "contemplative" ... tradi-
> tion in the Church than a kind of gnosticism which
> would elevate the contemplative above the ordinary
> Christian by initiating him into a realm of esote-
> ric knowledge and experience, delivering him from
> the ordinary struggles and sufferings of human
> existence ....[41]

In other terms, if contemplation is seen as "a static
awareness of metaphysical essences apprehended as spiritual objects" (V 17, TS2) or as some kind of gnostic
"ability to read the secrets of men's hearts" (V 24,
TS2), it can never command the interest of any but a
religious elite. But if it is "the experiential grasp
of reality as subjective" (V 21, TS2: emphasis Merton's),
or an "awakening to the Real within all that is real"
(V 15, TS2), then it can be offered without embarrassment to the whole human race.

This is precisely what Merton does in Ch. 39, a
chapter carefully named "The General Dance" (emphasis
mine). Merton in this final chapter presents contemplation in terms of the recovery of Paradise, the recovery
of the spiritual destiny of the sons and daughters of
Adam and Eve. "The world," he says, "was not made as a
prison for fallen spirits .... The world was made as a
temple, a paradise, into which God Himself would descend
to dwell familiarly with the spirits he had placed there
to tend it for Him" (V 482, TS2). In Genesis, he reminds
us, the whole inhabited earth, or the whole earth as an
inhabited place, i.e., the oikoumene, is depicted as a
garden (Persian pairidaeza, Hebrew pardès, Greek paradei-
sos, all meaning a garden set apart for the king's pleasure[42]) in which God may take delight (Hebrew eden, "delight"). In this garden God placed the spiritual beings
which he had created to share in his own divine tending
of creation: the human being was to be "the gardener of
paradise" (V 482, TS2). Once again, through contemplation,
God, Adam and Eve can walk together in Paradise Regained
in the cool of the day (Genesis 3.8), united without the
use of "words, or syllables or forms" (V 483, TS2). In

a great mystery, perhaps the deepest mystery of contemplative life, it is not so much that the true self of the
contemplative "has realized he is empty, ... has acquired
emptiness or become empty. He just 'is empty from the beginning, as Dr. Suzuki has observed."[43] In a bewildering
contemplative time-warp, the fall has never occurred, and
all the damage done by sin since (and not since) the fall
(non-fall) has been obliterated (needed no obliteration).
This in no way denies the atonement, nor "the economy of
sacraments, charity and the Cross,"[44] however: in effect,
it extends our common view of the power of the atonement
backward by grace to the time before the fall (cf. 1 Peter
3.18-20).

The incarnation is then seen in this paradisaical
context as the all-inclusive and eternal act of God by
which God "became not only Jesus Christ but also poten-
tially every man and woman that ever existed" (V 485, NSC),
and thereby the means of unity beyond all the dualities,
unity between God and God's children in the garden. The
paradisaical perspective, then, is incarnational as well
as creational; and a sophianic invitation is extended
to anyone who understands and accepts this.

> The presence of God in His world as its Creator de-
> pends on no one but Him. His presence in the world
> as Man, depends, in some measure, upon men. Not
> that we can do anything to change the mystery of
> the Incarnation in itself: but we are able to de-
> cide whether we ourselves, and that portion of the
> world which is ours, shall become aware of His pre-
> sence, consecrated by it, and transfigured in its
> light (V 486, TS2).

We can learn something of what this sophianic and paradisaical consecration of one's world meant for Merton him-

self when we look at the point vierge passages in Conjectures. Merton, of course, as a monk of Gethsemani, arose
at 2.15 am at the summons of the monastery bells. In this
passage he describes the part of the night before true
dawn, the point vierge of the diurnal cycle. He pictures
the birds[45] asking God

> if it is time for them to "be." He answers "yes."
> Then, they one by one wake up, and become birds.
> They manifest themselves as birds, beginning to
> sing. Presently they will be fully themselves,
> and will even fly.
>
> Meanwhile, the most wonderful moment of the day
> is that when creation in its innocence asks permis-
> sion to "be" once again, as it did on the first
> morning that ever was. ...
>
> Here is an unspeakable secret: paradise is
> all around us and we do not understand. It is wide
> open. The sword is taken away ....[46]

The contemplative meets this moment of the primordial and
divine "yes" with the "yes" of his/her own freedom.[47]
It is, on a daily basis, "a return in spirit to the first
morning of the world,"[48] a return made each day by the
contemplative who consecrates his/her own space and time
to the victory of Christ which has come to him/her
through Sophia.

> It is like the first morning of the world (when
> Adam, at the voice of Wisdom, awoke from nonentity
> and knew her), and like the Last Morning of the
> world when all the fragments of Adam will return
> from death at the voice of Hagia Sophia ....[49]

In the meantime, and under the rubric of this daily sophianic consecration, the contemplative responds to the

voice of God calling him/her to come and play in the garden of Paradise, to join the Creator in the cosmic dance.
This dance, as we have noted, is <u>general</u>, not just religious, not even simply Christian, nor, more specifically
still, Roman Catholic and monastic (the stance of the
early versions).[50] With Chs. 1 and 2 and Ch. 39 as pillars
of the frame, all the smaller shifts of tone and language
throughout the revisions can now be seen to hold a support-
ive or bracing position. Within this framework, the original material of TS1, amended and expanded, has been
purged of elitism and is now presented to anyone concerned
with "the Real within all that is real" (V 15, TS2).

Perhaps the nub of the difference between the early
versions and the final text can be imaged by a juxtaposi-
tion of the two metaphors which Merton uses to epitomize
the "depths of wide open darkness" (V 371, TS1) in which
contemplation is experienced. "And in the midst of you"
Merton had written first of all in TS1, "they form a citadel":[51] but in NSC, the citadel has become "a wide, impregnable country."[52] Both are images of security in the
life of the spirit; but the first suggests enclosure,
the second openness and freedom. In the citadel dwells
one inhabitant, the empirical ego, the objective self,
nourished on knowledge. In the wide country of innocence,
there is room for an infinite number in the holy common-
wealth of contemplation. This is "the true society of charity" where together "all find Paradise, which is the
sharing of [Christ's] love for His Father in the Person
of Their Spirit" (V 112, NSC).[53] The wide country is in
fact Paradise recovered; for without the fall, the earthly
Paradise would, according to patristic thought, have been
able to contain the total number of the descendants of
Adam and Eve, which, in mystical truth, it still can.[54]

This contrast in image suggests to me that at some
point between the editing of SCR in 1949 and the writing
of TS2 and NSC in 1960-61, Merton himself reached the
point vierge about which he writes so movingly and con-
vincingly, and found that what appeared from the outside
looking in to be a citadel, appeared from the inside looking out to be the center of a wide country. He made this
discovery without moving from this metaphysical center,
but simply turning around where he was, so to speak, 180
degrees. As Sally Fitzgerald writes (with no reference to
this particular passage), Merton's

> cell window in the Abbey close had opened into wide
> vistas of natural beauty, human experience, and
> divine reality, all of which he would convey to us
> vividly in his books.[55]

The difference is not one of location but of perspective.
I would suggest that it was Merton's own strong sense of
contemplative vocation that drew him towards the citadel
and finally into it, requiring as it did that "mystical
death" without which there is "no advance into the promised land of mystical union" (V 339, TS2);[56] that it
was his existential sickness, following so soon after he
reached the final institutional goal of ordination,[57] and
his profound psychic self-emptying in the publication of
his autobiography, together with the need to recover from
the "mystical death," which turned him around in it; and
that it was his work as pastor, teacher of students and
novices, and correspondent--his "contact with other soli-
tudes" (V 8, TS2)--which showed him at last that what he
had thought was a citadel was in fact the center of an
infinite realm.

These two images of the citadel and the wide country

arise, it seems to me, out of Merton's personal sense of
"place" in the world. When he wrote TS1, SC and SCR, Gethsemani was his citadel, his paradisus claustralis, his
Eden regained, his home.[58] The Sign of Jonas as a whole
is a celebration of the stability in both the monastic
and personal senses which he then believed himself to have
found at Gethsemani.[59] But in the mid-fifties his orientation shifted, as I have indicated, 180 degrees. Woodcock
makes the same point when he says that by the time of Conjectures, Merton was "at last looking from the monastic
enclosure outward at the world rather than from the monastic enclosure inward at the self,"[60] as he had done in
Jonas. He was de-romanticizing the monastic institution
and simultaneously feeling the resurgence of the old impulse to deep solitude. Suffocated to some extent by the
routines of community life, he yet saw no point in leaving. Thus by the time of TS2/NSC, seeing himself at the
center of the wide country, he did not wish to leave
Gethsemani (canonically, at least: he was always looking,
in his last years, for a more solitary location for his
hermitage), any more than he would have wished to leave
Paradise. But Paradise/Gethsemani, instead of being the
terminus of his contemplative quest, now became the base
for his life as a contemplative in the world of action.
The texture of his own life and heart had taught him ex-
perientially the truth of Cassian's statement that the
recovery of Paradise is only the "intermediate end of
the spiritual life."[61] On his way to it, however (and
while writing TS1, SC and SCR he was still very much "on
the way"[62]), it appeared to be the final goal. Once
reached, it then revealed itself to him as literally in-
termediate--between the alienated world which he had left,
and the Kingdom of God towards which he was pressing (cf.

Philippians 3.13, where occurs the only NT incidence of
epekteinomenos, a participial form derived from epekteino,
"I stretch out farther, reach out towards, strain for,"
and to epektasis, "extension, stretching out," especially
in time).[63] His entry into the hermitage in 1965 was the
concrete vocational expression of what was happening to
him inwardly. He was taking his distance from the monastic
institution, yet without rejecting it, any more than he
rejected scholasticism when he embarked on his exploration
of Zen. The recovery of Paradise, he had discovered, was
penultimate and intermediate; only the Kingdom of God
could be, for the mature contemplative, ultimate and immediate.

Once accomplished, this shift in perspective points
out the consistent direction of the rest of Merton's life,
the direction followed through many interests and ever-
widening circles of relationship, which eventually took
him, but with no sense of any further shift as basic as
this one, to Bangkok. I cannot therefore agree with his
statement in the preface to New Seeds that "it does not
matter whether or not many read the second version" (V 9),
"second version" here meaning the final text of New Seeds,
not SCR. I must agree instead with Aldhelm Cameron-Brown,
who remarks that "At first glance, New Seeds is simply
a revision of Seeds. But the alterations and additions
are revealing ...."[64]--as we have seen. So it is important that anyone coming to Merton for what he has to give
should not simply remain with the early Merton of TS1/SC/
SCR in the citadel,[65] but should open his or her eyes,
as on the first morning of creation, and find himself/her-
self in Paradise, in the wide and impregnable country of
the spirit, in the motionless ecstasy of the general dance.

For the world and time are the dance of the Lord in
emptiness. The silence of the spheres is the music
of a wedding feast. The more we persist in misunder-
standing the phenomena of life, the more we analyze
them out into strange finalities and complex purposes
of our own, the more we involve ourselves in sadness,
absurdity and despair. But it does not matter much,
because no despair of ours can alter the reality of
things, or stain the joy of the cosmic dance which
is always there. Indeed, we are in the midst of it,
and it is in the midst of us, for it beats in our
very blood, whether we want it to or not.

Yet the fact remains that we are invited to
forget ourselves on purpose, cast our awful solemnity to the winds and join in the general dance
(V 488, NSC).

Beyond the manifest beauty of this passage as printed,
there is something wonderful, it seems to me, in the fact
that at the end of so profound a book, in what was probably
his last editorial emendation, Merton could add the words
"cast our awful solemnity to the winds." If our solemnity
is oppressing us (or others), then we have not yet become
still enough, in God, to feel in ourselves the pulse of
the dance, and to respond to it by the depth of our
living and of our joy.

*

And so to conclude.

Our purpose in this study has been to trace and to
document something of the growth of Thomas Merton as
Christian contemplative and as spiritual theologian between 1948 and 1961. This has been possible, in the first

place, on the basis of the variorum edition of the five
fundamental texts which culminated in New Seeds of Contemplation; and in the second place, by an examination and interpretation of variant readings within the work considered
as one whole. We have discovered that the man who when he
wrote his autobiography believed that his spiritual journey had ended had travelled very much farther, becoming
in the process very much the same kind of ikon of Christian
wholeness to his own age that Bernard of Clairvaux had
been to his. Having fled from the world in anger, self-
reproach and confusion, he had returned to it in love
and compassion, with the recovery of Paradise through contemplation serving both as the medium of this final conversion and as his message to the world of action in which
we all must live. Glenn Hinson provides us with a last
comment, which epitomizes both this process as well as
Merton's significance as a spiritual theologian in our
time.

> In a remarkable way Merton put together the whole
> essential corpus of the Church's teaching on prayer.
> The one element which he added as the bond of it all
> was himself. The fact that he was engaged in this
> during a revolutionary era assured that he too would
> evolve in his understanding of prayer. This evolution
> can be portrayed in terms of a spiral outwards to
> encompass an ever larger world. It was the catholi-
> cizing of contemplation which Merton gave as his
> unique gift.[66]

It is to this process of catholicizing, of generous sharing
with the rest of the human race, that Merton's revision of
his contemplative testimony in the documents of our study
bears eloquent and persuasive witness.

NOTES

[1]For an account of his death, see "Letter to Abbot Flavian Burns," The Asian Journal of Thomas Merton, ed. Naomi Burton et. al. (New York: New Directions, 1973), 343-47. His death was marked by a number of unusual circumstances which I have detailed in "Thomas Merton and Bangkok: The Zen Death of a Christian Monk" (unpublished paper, 1976). The medical conclusion was that he died of "electric shock, or if you prefer, heart failure induced by electric shock" (Patrick Hart, rev. of Frank dell'Isola, Thomas Merton: A Bibliography, in "Bulletin of Monastic Spirituality," Cistercian Studies 10 (1975), item 422).

[2]Contemplative Prayer (New York: Herder, 1969), historical studies; My Argument with the Gestapo (Garden City, NY: Doubleday, 1969), an autobiographical novel; The Geography of Lograire (New York: New Directions, 1969), an unfinished anti-epic; Opening the Bible (Collegeville, MN: Liturgical Press, 1971), a general intro- duction; Thomas Merton on Peace, ed. Gordon Zahn (New York: McCall, 1971), rpt. as The Nonviolent Alternative (New York: Farrar, Straus and Giroux, 1980), an anthology; Contemplation in a World of Action, introd. Jean Leclercq (Garden City: Doubleday, 1971), articles on monastic renewal; He Is Risen (Niles, IL: Argus, 1975), an Easter sermon; Ishi Means Man: Essays on the Native American Indian (Greens- boro, NC: Unicorn, 1976); The Asian Journal (see n. 1, above), the record of his Asian trip, extensively documented; The Collected Poems (New York: New Directions, 1977); The Monastic Journey, ed. Patrick Hart (Kansas City: Sheed, Andrews and McMeel, 1977), on monastic renewal; with Robert Lax, A Catch of Anti-Letters (Kansas City: Sheed, Andrews and McMeel, 1978), letters 1962-67; Love and Living, ed. Naomi Burton and Patrick Hart (New York: Farrar, Straus and Giroux, 1979), essays; Thomas Merton on St Bernard (Kalamazoo, MI: Cistercian Publications, 1980), collected articles; The Literary Essays (New York: New Directions, 1981); Introductions East & West, ed. Robert E. Daggy (Greensboro: Unicorn, 1981), Merton's foreign prefaces; Wood, Shore, Desert, ed. Joel Weishaus (Santa Fe: Museum of New Mexico Press, 1982), a journal of 1968. (I have omitted some smaller items of less general interest from this period.)

[3]Perhaps the best general book on Merton to date is George Woodcock, Thomas Merton: Monk and Poet (Vancouver: Douglas & McIn- tyre, 1978). Marquita Breit, Thomas Merton: A Bibliography (Metuchen, NJ: Scarecrow Press/ATLA, 1974), covers the period 1957-73 for both

primary and secondary sources. Frank dell'Isola, Thomas Merton: A Bibliography (New York: Farrar, Straus and Cudahy, 1956), covers the period up to and including 1956 for both primary and secondary materials. A rev. ed. (Kent, OH: Kent State University Press, 1975) restricts itself to primary sources only. The Merton Seasonal, ed. Robert E. Daggy (Louisville, KY: Thomas Merton Studies Center, 1975-), contains a running bibliography. The authorized biography, originally entrusted to John Howard Griffin, has since his death been handed over to Michael Mott: publication, by Houghton Mifflin, is expected in the fall of 1984 or later.

4(Philadelphia: Fortress Press, 1976), p. xx.

5Capps, 155.

6John Eudes Bamberger interprets this dialectical aspect of Merton in "The Monk," in Patrick Hart, ed., Thomas Merton/Monk (New York: Sheed and Ward, 1974), 37-58. Merton himself refers to the paradoxical character of his life on numerous occasions.

7Continuum 7 (1969), the summer issue. Daniel Berrigan, in Portraits of Those I Love (New York: Crossroad, 1982), calls him "a friend peerless among friends" (14).

8E. Glenn Hinson, "Merton's Many Faces," Religion in Life 42 (1973), 153-67.

9Hart, ed., Thomas Merton/Monk.

10On this, see E. Glenn Hinson, "The Catholicizing of Contemplation: Thomas Merton's Place in the Church's Prayer Life," Cistercian Studies 10 (1975), 173; and John F. Teahan, "A Dark and Empty Way: Thomas Merton and the Apophatic Tradition," Journal of Religion 58 (1978), 284.

11Pray to Live: Thomas Merton, A Contemplative Critic (Notre Dame, IN: Fides, 1972), 14.

12"The Spiritual Writer," in Hart, ed., Thomas Merton/Monk, 122.

13Introd., Contemplation in a World of Action, 18.

14"Thomas Merton: Symbol and Synthesis of Contemporary Catholicism," Cistercian Studies 12 (1977), 283.

15"Thomas Merton: The Pursuit of Marginality," Christian Century 95 (6 December 1978), 1183.

[16]Teahan, 284.

[17]"Thomas Merton: An Appraisal," American Benedictine Review 18 (1967), 226. On the negative side, see Sebastian Moore and Kevin Maguire, The Dreamer not the Dream (New York: Newman, 1977, cop. 1970): "Thomas Merton is now unreadable. His spirituality now appears as a romanticised scholasticism, in which the entities of scholastic philosophy ... were clothed in flesh and blood and made the participants in an emotionally involving drama" (77-78). Comments of this kind, frequently encountered in conversations about Merton, are only very occasionally found in print. In my view, those making them are thereby giving evidence that they have not followed Merton through the full progress of his spiritual development.

[18]On this, see Cunningham, 1181; Hinson, "The Catholicizing of Contemplation," 173; Teahan, "Meditation and Prayer in Merton's Spirituality," ABR 30 (1979) 107.

[19]"... un signe pour nous de ce que doit être le chrétien de l'avenir"--"Le voyage du pèlerin: la vie de Thomas Merton," Esprit 38 (1970), 460. Cf. Merton: "Every monk, in whom Christ lives, and in whom the prophecies are therefore fulfilled, is a witness and a sign of the Kingdom of God"--The Sign of Jonas (Garden City, NY: Doubleday, 1956, cop. 1953), 20.

[20]Cunningham, 1183.

[21]"Thomas Merton within a Tradition of Prayer," Cistercian Studies 13 (1978), 377.

[22]Malits, "Symbol and Synthesis," 285. Teahan elsewhere makes the same point: see "Renunciation of Self and World: A Critical Dialectic in Thomas Merton," Thought 53 (1978), 150.

[23]Malits, "Symbol and Synthesis," 285.

[24]Loc. cit.

[25]Elena Malits, "'To Be What I Am': Thomas Merton as a Spiritual Writer," in Gerald Twomey, ed., Prophet in the Belly of a Paradox (New York: Paulist, 1978), 198; cf. Jonas, 313, par. 2.

[26]Conjectures of a Guilty Bystander (Garden City: Doubleday, 1968, cop. 1966), 338-39.

[27]Ibid., 339.

[28]See Charles Dumont, "A Contemplative at the Heart of the

World: Thomas Merton," Lumen Vitae 24 (1969), 633-46.

[29] Contrasting the vocations to social ministry and contemplation, Aldhelm Cameron-Brown remarks: "My neighbor is indeed an icon
of God; but then, so is my self, in a different way or, rather, offering a different approach" ("Zen Master," in Hart, ed., Thomas
Merton/Monk, 163). (I use the spelling "ikonic" to agree with Merton's usage.)

[30] Cf. Brother Marc, "The Monk: Icon of Christ," Monastic Ex-
change 9.3-4 (1977), 10-14.

[31] On the Cistercian "image" tradition, see Louis Bouyer, The
Cistercian Heritage (Westminster, MD: Newman, 1958, cop. 1955), 53;
and Gerald Twomey, "The Doctrine of the Human Person as Image of
God in the Writings of Thomas Merton," Cistercian Studies 13 (1978),
216-23.

[32] On his personal qualities, see Malits, "'To Be What I Am,'"
199; Matthew Kelty, "The Man," in Hart, Thomas Merton/Monk, 19-35;
and Bamberger, "The Monk," ibid., 37-58.

[33] Many critics emphasize this; see, for example, D. K. Swearer,
"Three Modes of Zen Buddhism in America," Journal of Ecumenical
Studies 10 (1973), 301.

[34] "A Model for Assessing Thomas Merton's Significance," Cistercian Studies 13 (1978), 379.

[35] "The Catholicizing of Contemplation," 189.

[36] "Merton and the East," Cistercian Studies 13 (1978), 310.

[37] Cf. Bamberger: "The full meaning of a man's life and the
breadth of his character appear only with the flow of time when the
seeds of new and hidden forms of life planted by his hand have been
able to appear and flower. In the case of Thomas Merton the sheer
mass of his writings poses formidable problems to anyone who would
attempt to present his thought to the world. The fact that only a
small fraction of the fifteen journals he wrote have been published
and only a few of the several thousands of letters--some of them
veritable treatises, and all of them containing important information
for understanding his rich and complex personality--makes it impossible
to achieve anything like a definitive portrait of the man or sketch
of his thought at this time" (in his preface to Nouwen, Pray to Live,
p. viii).

[38] Matthew Kelty, one of his brothers at Gethsemani, gives us

a description of his method, which normally involved an initial typescript, two re-readings and the insertion of handwritten alterations,
a second typing, and final editorial revisions. "His biggest problem,"
says Kelty, was "keeping things limited, for the more he worked on
a script the bigger it got. He kept getting new insights, new openings"
("The Man," 21).

[39] Not simply eulogic, "universal man" refers to the term of
the process of "final integration," in the phrase of Iranian psyci-
atrist A. R. Arasteh. For Merton on this, see his "Final Integration:
Toward a 'Monastic Therapy,'" Contemplation in a World of Action,
219-31. See also W. M. Thompson, "Merton's Contribution to a Transcultural Consciousness," in Donald Grayston and Michael W. Higgins,
eds., Thomas Merton: Pilgrim in Process (Toronto: Griffin House, 1983),
147-69.

[40] Raymond Bailey quotes Dan Walsh as saying that The Seven
Storey Mountain (New York: Harcourt, Brace, 1948) was Merton's
"purest mystical work"--Thomas Merton on Mysticism (Garden City:
Doubleday, 1975), 78.

[41] As he notes on the last page of Seeds.

[42] Dell'Isola, Bibliography, rev. ed., 9.

[43] Jonas, 226.

[44] He takes the phrase from Louis Massignon: see Conjectures,
151, cf. 131, 158. See also M. Madeline Abdelnour, "'Le point vierge'
in Thomas Merton," Cistercian Studies 6 (1971), 153-71.

[45] Cf. Giannini, 379. Giannini uses Toynbee's model of with-
drawal, transfiguration and return to illuminate the fundamental
movement in Merton's life.

[46] On his "Carthusian" temptations, see Jonas, 20, 67-68, 102,
127, 139, 244; and Conjectures, 183, 258. For a more general study,
see Richard Cashen, Solitude in the Thought of Thomas Merton (Kalamazoo, MI: Cistercian Publications, 1981).

[47] "First and Last Thoughts: An Author's Preface," in Thomas P.
McDonnell, ed., A Thomas Merton Reader, rev. ed. (Garden City: Doubleday, 1974), 15.

[48] Textual Variation and Theological Development in Thomas Merton's "Seeds of Contemplation" and "New Seeds of Contemplation," unpublished master's thesis (Toronto: Trinity College/TST, 1974).

[49] On the Seeds page of the first draft of this catalogue, completed by Sr Thérèse in 1962 and sent to Merton for his annotations, he comments: "There is a holograph in small notebooks, rather different from the typed version. I gave it to Clare Boothe Luce & she said she was giving it to the monastery at Mepkin in South Carolina. It may be there" (from a xerox in my possession, unpaginated). In the course of correspondence, I learned from Mrs Luce that the notebooks were not in her possession (letter, 3 June 1976), and from the Trappist community at Mepkin that they were not in theirs (letters, 11 January 1976 and 17 May 1976). Subsequent enquiries to libraries and to other persons suggested by Br Patrick Hart, Merton's secretary in the year before his death, produced no clues; nor did letters to the editor printed in Christian Century 94 (26 January 1977), 262, and in Commonweal 104 (1 April 1977), 223. In the event of their turning up, they could be correlated with the variorum text. Merton's statement in the preface to A Thomas Merton Reader that he wrote Seeds in 1947 ("First and Last Thoughts," 15) may be another reference to this holograph text.

[50] I took the idea of comparing Seeds and New Seeds from a suggestion of Bertrand de Margerie, "L'insertion du Moi et du Nous dans la vie contemplative, selon Thomas Merton," Science et Esprit 22 (1970), 316. Mark Gibbard speaks of comparing them "almost in the way New Testament students compare the synoptic gospels in parallel columns"--"The Friend I Never Met," Cistercian Studies 13 (1978), 397.

[51] The Waters of Siloe (New York: Harcourt, Brace, 1949, rpt. Garden City: Doubleday, 1962); The New Man (New York: Farrar, Straus and Cudahy, 1962, rpt. London: Burns, Oates, 1976).

[52] I make no attempt, except in the most general way, to identify or discuss Merton's sources. This would be an enormous and delicate enterprise beyond the scope of this study. On this problem, see Teahan, "A Dark and Empty Way," 267.

Chapter 2/Merton: A Biographical Hermeneutic

[1] Peter Kountz, "The Seven Storey Mountain of Thomas Merton," Thought 49 (1974), 250-67, is a valuable though somewhat flawed treatment. See also Donald Grayston, "Autobiography and Theology: The Once and Future Merton," in Grayston and Higgins, Thomas Merton: Pilgrim in Process, 71-84; and Woodcock, Thomas Merton, 22-23, 28-29, 62-66, 128-29.

[2] Edward Rice, The Man in the Sycamore Tree (Garden City: Doubleday, 1970), 64.

[3]Cameron-Brown, 162.

[4]Ibid., 163.

[5]Rice, 63. See also Thérèse Lentfoehr, "The Spiritual Writer," 107-08; and cf. Richard Lovelace, who testifies: "... I was initially converted to Christianity from atheism through reading Thomas Merton's Seven Storey Mountain and ... my effort here (which in so many other ways parallels Merton's) strives in the same direction he was traveling in his later years"--Dynamics of Spiritual Life: An Evangelical Theology of Renewal (Downers Grove, IL: Inter-Varsity Press, 1979), 17.

[6]Leclercq, introd., Contemplation in a World of Action, 9.

[7]Rice, 65. Numbers one and two were The White Collar Zoo and a book on canasta: Twomey, Prophet, 12.

[8]It is because of this phrase, "under the sign of the Water Bearer," that I have called this statement "astrological." From my reading of Merton, it seems likely that this reference to Aquarius is an oblique and proleptic reference to his baptism as a Roman Catholic, and to Christ as the divine bearer of the living water of the Spirit (see Mountain, 221-25).

[9]Mountain, 3.

[10]Ibid., 10.

[11]Ibid., 5.

[12]Ibid., 9.

[13]Ibid., 19.

[14]On his literary interests, see Herbert C. Burke, "The Man of Letters," Continuum 7 (1969), 274-85.

[15]Merton retained his interest in Blake to the end of his life; see his article, "Blake and the New Theology," Sewanee Review 76 (1968), 673-82. See also Michael W. Higgins, "A Study of the Influence of William Blake on Thomas Merton," ABR 25 (1974), 377-88.

[16]Mountain, 124-25. Ross Labrie suggests that the young woman at Cambridge who may have borne Merton's child "underlies the scandalized reaction of Merton's guardian at the end of the year at Cambridge": The Art of Thomas Merton (Fort Worth, TX: Texas Christian University Press, 1979), 40.

[17] Woodcock, 11.

[18] Of the book-length studies so far, Nouwen's has the approbation of Merton's monastic brothers, as does Woodcock's. Rice's does not, probably because in their view it makes unsubstantiated claims and distorts Merton's sense of humor into literalism. An overstressing of the tensions between Merton and James Fox, Gethsemani's abbot for most of Merton's time is their major objection to Monica Furlong, Merton: A Biography (San Francisco: Harper and Row, 1980). On this, see Bamberger, "In Search of Thomas Merton," CS 17 (1982), 99-109.

[19] Labrie calls the Columbia years "fertile and restless" (47).

[20] Nouwen, 25.

[21] Mountain, 140.

[22] On Walsh, see Mountain, 259-65; on Lax, ibid., 179-81, 236-38, cf. Jonas, 313.

[23] Mountain, 191-98.

[24] On Gilson, see Mountain, 171-75; on Huxley, ibid., 184-87; on John of the Cross, ibid., 186, 238; on Ignatius, ibid., 268-70.

[25] Mountain, 223.

[26] A recurrent metaphor in the early years: see Mountain, 164, 203.

[27] Another metaphor for the same reality: see Mountain, 350, 352.

[28] Quoted in Rice, 48.

[29] Mountain, 297-98. Nouwen says that the Franciscans rejected Merton in a "discourteous manner" (9), but I have found no written evidence in Merton to this effect.

[30] The Secular Journal (Garden City: Doubleday, 1969, cop. 1959), 167.

[31] Not 1942, as Nouwen says (9).

[32] At St Bonaventure, when he was trying to make a final decision about his vocation, he "heard" the bell of Gethsemani, "calling me home" (Mountain, 365). From his first visit, it wa his home.

[33] See Jonas, 119, and Hart, Thomas Merton/Monk, 126.

³⁴Jonas, 319-21. J. T. Baker sees this event as one of the major reasons why Merton turned in the fifties to social criticism and the struggle for justice: "The Social Critic," Continuum 7 (1969), 263.

³⁵A. M. Allchin, "The Importance of One Good Place," CS 14 (1979), 93-97.

³⁶Quoted in Twomey, "The Struggle for Racial Justice," in Twomey, ed., Prophet, 93; cf. Labrie, 68.

³⁷"A Homily," Continuum 7 (1969), 226.

³⁸Jonas, 312.

³⁹"First and Last Thoughts," 15.

⁴⁰Jonas, 181. In all probability, he would now have chosen to be a simple monk rather than a priest as well. On this, see F. J. Kelly, Man Before God (Garden City: Doubleday, 1974), 42-48.

⁴¹See on this Bamberger, "The Monk," 48.

⁴²Jonas, 226.

⁴³Nouwen, 45.

⁴⁴Ibid., 46.

⁴⁵Loc. cit.

⁴⁶Jonas, 261.

⁴⁷Thérèse Lentfoehr, "Thomas Merton: The Dimensions of Solitude," ABR 23 (1972), 346.

⁴⁸Thomas Merton, Disputed Questions (Toronto: New American Library of Canada, 1965, cop. 1960), 146-47.

⁴⁹Jonas, 261.

⁵⁰"First and Last Thoughts," 16-17.

⁵¹Jonas, 229.

⁵²Ibid., 226.

⁵³Contemplation in a World of Action, 228; cf. Ch. 1, n. 39.

[54]From this point on, says Hinson, Merton found himself able "to unite all things to Christ in and through his own person"--"Merton's Many Faces," 159.

[55]Conjectures, 144.

[56]Ibid., 21.

[57]"The Monk," 40.

[58]"First and Last Thoughts," 17.

[59]Asian Journal, pp. xxi-xxii, 326-43.

[60]Ibid., 100-02, 112-13, 124-25.

[61]Patrick Hart, in his "Postscript" to the Asian Journal, tells how the community of Gethsemani learned of Merton's death (257-59).

[62]The Seduction of the Spirit (New York: Simon and Schuster, 1973), 9.

[63]Sallie McFague TeSelle, "An 'Intermediary' Theology: In Service of the Hearing of God's Word," Christian Century 92 (25 June 1975), 625-29.

[64]Sallie McFague TeSelle, Speaking in Parables (Philadelphia: Fortress, 1975), 4.

[65]Biography as Theology (Nashville: Abingdon, 1974), 37.

[66]Ibid., 96-97.

[67]Ibid., 89-90.

[68]Ibid., 102.

[69]"'To Be What I Am,'" 197.

[70]"Symbol and Synthesis," 283.

[71]"Thomas Merton: Monk and Author," in Twomey, 144.

[72]In John S. Dunne's view, this is the person who "passes over by sympathetic understanding from his own religion to other religions and comes back again with new insight to his own"--The Way of All the Earth (New York: Macmillan, 1972), p. ix.

[73]See, on this, Teahan, "A Dark and Empty Way," 284.

[74]"Merton's Metaphors: Signs and Sources of Spiritual Growth," CS 13 (1978), 334.

[75]Jonas, 166. Earlier in Jonas he had stated that interior events "usually keep pace with exterior events of one kind or another" (18), in a kind of sacramental way. His focus in Jonas, as in most of his writing, was not upon doctrines as such, but on "their repercussions in the life of a soul in which they begin to find a concrete realization" (loc. cit.).

Chapter 3/TS1: Seeds in Typescript

[1]Sr Thérèse did not know the whereabouts of the missing portions, a total of 14 pages (personal conversation).

[2](Springfield, IL: Templegate, 1978, cop. 1948), 16-17. I am indebted to William H. Shannon, Thomas Merton's Dark Path: The Inner Experience of a Contemplative (New York: Penguin, 1982, cop. 1981), for these connections: see especially 506, 34-35.

[3]Contemplation in a World of Action, 30.

[4]Together with "wound" and "exile," "contradiction" is a metaphor pointing to the basic human reality of alienation. Ch. 2 of the second part of the Mountain, for example, "The Waters of Contradiction," describes his backsliding after baptism. In terms of the TS1 quotation, he did not yet "perfectly" love God.

[5]Mountain, 3.

[6]The three paragraphs which follow this statement in TS1 are omitted in SC. They relate this thought of God being found within the person to various NT scriptures (Gal 2.19, Rom 8.11. 2 Pet 2.12), and to what he had said earlier about the "missions" of God (cf. V 64-68).

[7]Mountain, 221; see also 222-25.

[8]Ibid., 228.

[9]Loc. cit.

[10]Conjectures, 156-57. Gibbard sees this experience as no less than a "second conversion" ("The Friend I Never Met," 397).

[11]On Merton's usefulness to laypeople, see Kenneth C. Russell, "Merton on the Lay Contemplative: Explicit Statements and Refracted Light," in Grayston and Higgins, 121-31.

[12]On this see Kelty, "The Man," 24.

[13]Seduction of the Spirit, 67.

[14]As regards these early contacts of Merton with "Protestant-ism," see, on the lycée, Mountain, 32-33, 49-53; on the chaplain at Oakham, ibid., 73-74; and on the rector of the Episcopal Church in Douglaston, ibid., 175-77.

[15]Mountain, 73-74.

[16]See the numerous index references in Conjectures to Barth, Bonhoeffer and other Protestant writers.

[17]On the recent history of scholasticism within the Roman Catholic community, see T. Mark Schoof, A Survey of Catholic Theology 1800-1970, introd. E. Schillebeeckx (New York: Paulist/Newman, 1970).

[18]See, on this, his introd. to Amédée Hallier, The Monastic Theology of Aelred of Rievaulx (Spencer, MA: Cistercian Publications, 1969), pp. vii-viii.

[19]Gordon Zahn says that its amplification and publication in NSC marks, for Merton, "the crossing-over point from meditation to political application" ("Thomas Merton: Reluctant Pacifist," in Twomey, Prophet, 58).

[20]Mountain, 213-14.

[21]For this development, see Zahn, ibid., 58 ff., and in the same volume, James H. Forest, "Thomas Merton's Struggle with Peace-making," 15-54.

[22]Mountain, 75-76.

[23]On "darkness" and "emptiness," see Teahan, "A Dark and Empty Way," passim.

[24]Mountain, 208-09.

[25]Ibid., 209.

[26]Ibid., 85.

[27]See also V 221-22, with its undertones of Harlem; cf. Mountain, 340-49; on "Frank Swift," 141-48.

[28]Cf. Jonas, 197-98.

[29]Ibid., 261.

[30]Ibid., 323.

[31]Loc. cit. On "saved" and "lost," see also his brief addition in the final text, V 62, NSC.

[32]Jonas, 59.

[33]Ibid., 259.

[34]Ibid., 263.

[35]Ibid., 290.

[36]Ibid., 139.

[37]Ibid., 318.

[38]Ibid., 139.

[39]Cf. his earlier statement in the Mountain: "Did I know that my own sins were enough to have destroyed the whole of England and Germany? (128).

[40]Mountain, 237-38; cf. his dream of being a saint, Jonas, 313.

[41]Jonas, 229.

[42]Cf. ibid., 312, 261.

[43]"Action is charity looking outward to other men, and contemplation is charity drawn inward to its own divine source. Action is the stream, and contemplation is the spring"--No Man Is An Island (Garden City: Doubleday, 1967, cop. 1955), 65.

[44]Cf. the experience of Paul as suggested by 2 Cor 12.2-6.

[45]Cf. his initial reaction to Gethsemani. The passage continues with echoes of the Beatitudes, particularly of the "meek" of Matt 5.4.

[46]The Human Journey: Thomas Merton, Symbol of a Century (Garden City: Doubleday, 1982), 39.

Chapter 4/SC: The First Published Version

[1]This and all other bibliographical information in this section not otherwise credited is from Dell'Isola, Bibliography, 8-10.

[2]Emile Cailliet, rev. in Journal of Religion 29 (1949), 241.

[3]Jonas, 166.

[4]Loc. cit.

[5]Only What is Contemplation? had intervened.

[6]Among the more critical are those by Philip Burnham, "Renunciation and Salvation," New York Times Book Review (20 March 1949),
4; Y. H. Krikorian, "The Fruits of Mysticism," New Republic 28 (12
September 1949), 17-18; and Ann F. Wolfe, "Into the First Heaven
of Paradise," Saturday Review 32 (16 April 1949), 43.

[7]Cailliet, 242.

[8]"Silence Broken," TLS (23 December 1949), 845.

[9]Jonas, 166.

[10]"The Spiritual Writer," 108.

[11]He mentions having read these in preparation for his solemn
profession: Jonas, 40, cf. 306.

[12]Clifford Stevens opines that SC "replaced The Imitation of
Christ as a manual of meditation, at least for one generation of
Catholics" ("Thomas Merton: An Appraisal," 225). Curiously, since
the article appeared in 1965, Stevens takes no notice of NSC. In
any case, the claim is excessive, inasmuch as no one book (other
than the Bible) could even then be said to hold a place of primacy
in the devotions of an increasingly pluralistic Church.

[13]As late as March 1965, Merton was still calling the work
"only a collection of intuitions and hints, which seek rather to
suggest than to define" ("Preface to the [first and authorized]
Japanese Edition of Seeds of Contemplation," in Introductions
East & West, 71). It is not clear from this preface whether it
refers to a translation of SC or SCR.

[14]Stevens, 225.

[15] Discussing the <u>Mountain</u> on one occasion, Merton referred to it as a "legend," and added: "The legend is stronger than I am. Nevertheless, I rebel against it, and maintain my basic human right not to be turned into a Catholic myth for children in parochial schools"--Thomas P. McDonnell, "An Interview with Thomas Merton," <u>Motive</u> 27 (1967), 33, quoted in Kountz, 264.

[16] In <u>Conjectures</u>, he says that his illusion of monastic separateness from the world lasted "sixteen or seventeen years" (157).

[17] <u>Jonas</u>, 152.

[18] The heavily juridical "licitly" is omitted in NSC.

[19] See, e.g., <u>Mountain</u>, 321-22.

[20] Towards the end of the <u>Mountain</u>, he speaks of "my enemy, Thomas Merton .... There seems to be no reason why he should not write for magazines" (412)--he means according to his superiors.

[21] He may have thought it might be read in the community refectory: see <u>Jonas</u>, 201.

[22] "<u>Todo y Nada</u>: Writing and Contemplation," <u>Renascence</u> 2.2 (Spring 1950), 87-101.

[23] <u>Ibid</u>., 89.

[24] <u>Ibid</u>., 90.

[25] Rice, 19; see also Labrie, 40.

[26] On his relations with women see Furlong, 14-15, 297-306, 314.

[27] Cf. <u>Jonas</u>, 323.

Chapter 5/SCR: Seeds Revised

[1] This and other bibliographical information not otherwise credited is found in Dell'Isola, <u>Bibliography</u>, 9.

[2] In the library of Emmanuel College, Toronto.

[3] See Breit, <u>Bibliography</u>, items 143, 144, 147, 196.

[4]Woodcock, 93; Lentfoehr, "The Spiritual Writer," 114; Shannon, 34.

[5]Lentfoehr, loc. cit.

[6]See Dell'Isola, 163-80; Breit, item 904; Introductions, 132.

[7]Cf. his more mature "The Humanity of Christ in Monastic Prayer," Monastic Studies 2 (1964), 1-27.

[8]"Silence Broken," 845. My mistaken inference occurs in "The Making of a Spiritual Classic: Thomas Merton's Seeds of Contemplation and New Seeds of Contemplation," Studies in Religion/Sciences Religieuses 3 (1973-74), 346.

[9]Chalmers McCormick dates it definitively from this gift of Merton to Suzuki in 1959--"The Zen Catholicism of Thomas Merton," Journal of Ecumenical Studies 9 (1972), 804. Robert E. Daggy, in his introduction to Merton's "Christian Contemplation," says that Merton's interest in the East had been deepening, "by his own estimate, since at least 1956" (4).

[10]Mountain, 74-75.

[11]Ibid., 187-88.

[12]Conjectures, 144.

[13]See V 487, and Cameron-Brown's comment, 166.

[14]See Jonas, 296. But cf. also Faith and Violence (Notre Dame, IN: NDU Press, 1968), 151.

[15]Jonas, 254.

[16]See Jacques Maritain, The Person and the Common Good (New York: Scribner's, 1947); and Charles A. Fecher, The Philosophy of Jacques Maritain (New York: Greenwood Press, 1953), 156-67, 204-09. Merton and Maritain were for many years personal friends and correspondents. Papers from a symposium held to honor both will be found in the Fall 1981 issue of Cross Currents.

[17]Cf. his own comment: "No matter what perfection you predicate of Him, you have to add that your concept is only a pale analogy of the perfection that is in God, and that He is not literally what you conceive by that term" (V 203, SCR).

[18]H. A. Reinhold, rev. in Commonweal 50 (15 April 1949), 20.

[19]Kelly, p. xiii.

[20]*Mountain*, 316-17.

[21]*Ibid.*, 325.

[22]Bamberger, "The Monk," 37.

[23]See *Conjectures*, 179-80. I also see the "workaday fishing schooner" of his dream of the great swim as a symbol of the monastic institution, which although Merton and others had tried "in many ways to make it move" had only "moved a little," and from which he would sooner or later have to "strike out and swim" (*ibid.*, 30).

[24]"The Humanity of Christ in Monastic Prayer," 27.

[25]In his "Author's Note" found at the beginning of *No Man Is An Island*, he calls the book "a sequel to a previous volume called *Seeds of Contemplation*" (7). But as he makes clear on the same page, the later book is designed deal with subjects logically preliminary to *Seeds* and *Seeds Revised*, though published later.

Chapter 6/TS2: Amplifications and Additions

[1]From a xerox of this letter in my possession.

[2]As received, the inserts were in this order: 1, 20b, 21-27, final (35), 28-34, 2, 4-9, 9a, 10-20, 20a. The reader's report, TS2a, came at the end, after insert 20a.

[3]By the "second writing" he means TS2 (and NSC), not SCR.

[4]In NSC, he tightens up this last phrase, altering "any Church" to "the Church."

[5]Reinhold, rev. in *Commonweal*, 20.

[6]Possibly his correspondents: for his feelings about them, see *Jonas*, 130-31, 136.

[7]"To read this book one does not need to be a Christian; it is sufficient that one is a man, and that he has in himself the instinct for truth" ("Preface to the Japanese Edition of *Seeds of Contemplation*," 71): yet surely here he has NSC in mind.

[8]Cf. what I have already said about the "reminting" of con-

templation as canonical metaphor (31-33, above).

[9] On contemplation as resonant of the "philosophic elitism of Plato and Plotinus," see Contemplation in a World of Action, 173.

[10] Cf. also his use of consonantia as a metaphor of contemplative unity from the world of sound: "Day of a Stranger," Reader, 437.

[11] Cf. Jonas, 226.

[12] He continues, however, to assert the continuing need for theological study: see V 416-17.

[13] Merton's article "Final Integration," in Contemplation in a World of Action, gives evidence (228) that he saw in the approach to wholeness of A. R. Arasteh, an approach which had his whole-hearted approval, much in common with that of Jung. Sr Anne Saword, at the time co-editor of Cistercian Studies, informed me that another brother of Gethsemani had told her that Merton, just before leaving for Asia, had said that he planned to make Jung's works a major focus of study on his return (letter to the author, 17 January 1975).

[14] All the references to "worthiness" in the first part of insert 13 (V 124-26) were added by Merton after typing it; the second part of insert 13 (V 126-27) is a meditation on concern for "worthiness" as a characteristic of the false self of "every weak, lost and isolated member of the human race" (V 124).

[15] Merton's sense of God's mercy was very deep: cf. Mountain, 422, Jonas, 351-52. See also Morgan Hanlon, "The Spirituality of Thomas Merton," Sisters Today 44 (1972), 198-210. Hanlon describes Merton's sense of the providential mercy of God as the "capstone" of his spirituality, a "profound, unswerving conviction of a specific, concrete, particular Providence at work in his life" (201).

[16] A curiously antiquated term at this remove, seeming to conflict in both direction and tone with what Merton is saying here.

[17] The text is that of NSC. In TS2, Merton had omitted "all" in the phrase "but above all," and "not" in the phrase "I pray not only." To make sense of the first two sentences quoted above, they were added in NSC. He also substituted "my own country" for "America," his first choice in TS2, perhaps to enable his readers in whatever country to make the appropriate connection with the lands of their own citizenship. On Merton's own citizenship, see Ch. 2, n. 34, above.

[18]In spite of television's role in creating antipathy to war, Merton's view of TV remained a bleak one: see V 143, cf. Faith and Violence (Notre Dame, In: NDU Press, 1968), 151.

[19]For a thorough treatment of Merton's thought on peace, see Thomas Merton on Peace, ed. and introd. Gordon Zahn, also republished and retitled as The Nonviolent Alternative.

[20]Padovano, The Human Journey, 30.

[21]See Mountain, p. 222. See also Ch. 2, nn. 26-28, above.

[22]See on this Bouyer, Cistercian Heritage, 94-102.

[23]On his correspondence with Ruether, see Furlong, 278-79, 297-306.

Chapter 7/NSC: The Contemporary Encheiridion

[1]For bibliographical information in this section not otherwise credited, see Dell'Isola, Bibliography, 34-35.

[2]For his feelings about death at this precise age, see Conjectures, 189.

[3]Dell'Isola, 85.

[4]In the rev. ed. of 1974, see 65-66, 276-82, 319-24, 426-30, 439-45 and 500-05.

[5]C. M. Cherian, Clergy Monthly 28 (1964), 195-96; Christopher Derrick, Life of the Spirit 18 (1963), 36-38; G. Fitzgibbon, The Month 31 (1964), 57-58; Sr Mary Gilbert, Sewanee Review 72 (1964), 715-18; Sr Mary Vianney, Ave Maria 95 (3 March 1962), 27-28; Desmond Schlegel, The Tablet 216 (15 December 1962), 1225-26; Michael J. Sweetman, Studies 52 (1963), 334-36.

[6]Gilbert, 718.

[7]Sweetman, 336.

[8]Fitzgibbon, 57-58.

[9]Cherian, 196.

[10]Cameron-Brown, 165-66.

[11]Conrad Hoover, "A Reading of Thomas Merton, Personal and Partial," Sojourners 7 (December 1978), 31. The publisher of NSC is of course New Directions, not Lippincott (as Hoover states).

[12]Woodcock, 92.

[13]"First and Last Thoughts," 15-16. On the famous graph of 6 February 1967 on which he rates his own works, Merton ranked it among his "better" ones: see Introductions, 126-27.

[14]The date of 1964 for the French and Spanish is Dell'Isola's; Breit gives 1963 for both, and 1968 for the Italian; see also Introductions, 135.

[15]On the translations, see Dell'Isola, 163-80; Breit, 63-81.

[16]Dell'Isola, 35.

[17]M. Romanus Penrose, Review for Religious 31 (1972), 889.

[18]On this subject, see Conjectures, 114-17; The New Man, 159.

[19]The Golden Epistle to the Carthusians of Mont-Dieu (London: Sheed and Ward, 1930), 106.

[20]On "sonship," see also Conjectures, 158, 177-78.

[21]On Merton and Jews, see Edward K. Kaplan, "Contemplative Inwardness and Prophetic Action: Thomas Merton's Dialogue with Judaism," in Grayston and Higgins, 85-105.

[22]Cailliet, 242.

[23]But see also Cameron-Brown to the contrary, 166.

[24]For the text, see Walter M. Abbot, ed., The Documents of Vatican II (New York: Herder/Assocation Press, 1966), 13, 85-96. On Merton and Vatican II, see Woodcock, 101-20.

[25]In Conjectures (see index), we find references to Berdyaev, Evdokimov, Staretz Sylvan and Theophane the Recluse.

[26]"Thomas Merton and the Christian East," in A. M. Allchin, ed., Theology and Prayer (London: Fellowship of St Alban and St Sergius, 1975), 73.

[27]"Bread in the Wilderness: The Monastic Ideal in Thomas Merton and Paul Evdokimov," Allchin, 91.

[28]"Hagia Sophia," Reader, 506.

[29]Ibid., 509.

[30]Williams, in Allchin, 91.

[31]"Hagia Sophia," 510.

[32]Conjectures, 195.

[33]"... un des sages du royaume" ("L'insertion du Moi et du Nous," 316).

[34]Conjectures, 194. By "Asia" he means Hinduism and Buddhism. Cf. the "If I ..." passages, ibid., 144, 21.

[35]Ibid., 211.

[36]Ibid., 212.

[37]"First and Last Thoughts," 16.

[38]Conjectures, 245.

[39]"The Catholicizing of Contemplation," 175.

[40]Conjectures, 291-92.

[41]Williams, 91.

[42]Cf. Conjectures, 211-12.

[43]Ibid., 194.

Chapter 8/The Recovery of Paradise

[1]"Wilderness and Paradise: Two Recent Studies," CS 2 (1967), 84. One of the books reviewed was George H. Williams, Wilderness and Paradise in Christian Thought (New York: Harper, 1962), of which I have made extensive use in this chapter.

[2]See Mountain, 122-23.

[3]Secular Journal, 169-70, 172.

[4]Woodcock sees the motif as a strong link between Merton and Chuang Tzu (159).

[5] On this see Anselm Stolz, The Doctrine of Spiritual Perfection (St Louis: Herder, 1938), 17-36, 107-32.

[6] Ibid., 28.

[7] Ibid., 32.

[8] See on this Bouyer, Cistercian Heritage, 80-85.

[9] "Its likeness will return when it comes back to the Word in Whose image it was made. But the return of the soul is its turning to the Word to be reformed by Him and made to conform to Him. And how is it to conform? In love" (Bouyer, 53).

[10] It was published in James Laughlin, ed., New Directions 17 (New York: New Directions, 1961), 81-101; rpt. in Thomas Merton, Zen and the Birds of Appetite (New York: New Directions, 1968), 116-33--the edition from which I quote in this study (hereafter, Zen); rpt. also in Reader, 481-88.

[11] Zen, 116.

[12] Ibid., 117.

[13] Williams, 91; cf. The New Man, passim.

[14] Zen, 120.

[15] Ibid., 121.

[16] Ibid., 127.

[17] Ibid., 128.

[18] Loc. cit. See also Woodcock, 92. If anyone doubts the relevance of this, I offer the following quotation. "Why not abolish nuclear weapons? Why not cleanse this small planet of these deadly poisons? Because we cannot. Mankind's nuclear innocence, once lost, cannot be regained. The discovery of nuclear weapons, like the discovery of fire itself, lies behind us on the trajectory of history: it cannot be undone. Even if all nuclear arsenals were destroyed, the knowledge of how to reinvent them would remain and could be put to use in any of a dozen or more nations"--Albert Carnesale et. al., Living with Nuclear Weapons (New York: Bantam, 1983), 5: emphasis mine.

[19] Zen, 129.

[20]Zen, 125; cf. G. H. Williams, 47, 49.

[21]Ibid., 130.

[22]Ibid., 129.

[23]Ibid., 131-32. On the fact that there is no "Kingdom" in Zen, see Alexander Lipski, Thomas Merton and Asia: His Quest for Utopia (Kalamazoo, MI: Cistercian Publications, 1983), 29, and Paul Tillich, Christianity and the Encounter of the World Religions (New York: Columbia University Press, 1963), 64-75.

[24]Zen, 132.

[25]Mountain, 171-75.

[26]Hinson, "The Catholicizing of Contemplation," 178.

[27]Mountain, 221, cf. Shannon, 204.

[28]Jonas, 208.

[29]Hinson, 178-79.

[30]See on this Conjectures, 203-08.

[31]Mountain, 220.

[32]Conjectures, 205.

[33]See especially Dennis McInerny, "Thomas Merton on Oriental Thought," CS 14 (1979), 60-61; and Silvio E. Fittipaldi, "Preying Birds: An Examination of Thomas Merton's Zen," Horizons 9.1 (Spring 1982), 37-46.

[34]Mountain, 198.

[35]Thomas Merton, Mystics and Zen Masters (New York: Delta, 1969), 13-18; see also Paul F. Knitter, "Thomas Merton's Eastern Remedy for Christianity's 'Anonymous Dualism,'" Cross Currents 31 (1981), 285-95.

[36]Woodcock, 166. Cf. the remark of Prof. David Eckel of the Center for the Study of World Religions at Harvard that in The Asian Journal we find "as sophisticated an encounter with the Buddhist tradition as is available in the West" (lecture, 2 February 1984).

[37]In a late article Merton wrote of himself, humorously, as

one "who has been exposed to scholastic ontology and has not recovered"--"Blake and the New Theology," Sewanee Review 76 (1968), 679.

[38] McInerny, 65.

[39] Conjectures, 285; see also 181, 265, and Lipski, 34-35.

[40] Zen, 131; cf. Shannon, 205.

[41] Contemplative Prayer, 23.

[42] On the paradisaical tradition, see Pierre Miquel and Jean-
Claude Sagne, "Paradis," in Dictionnaire de spiritualité (Paris: Beau-
chesne, 1983), fasc. 76-77, cols. 187-203.

[43] Zen, 129.

[44] Contemplative Prayer, 23.

[45] It is one of the characteristics of the shaman, in so-called
primitive religious contexts, to be able to communicate with the
birds and animals, as in the time before the fall: see Mircea Eliade,
"Nostalgia for Paradise in the Primitive Traditions," in Myths, Dreams
and Mysteries (New York: Harper, 1960), 59-72; cf. Merton's comment
on the monk as someone with "a special kind of kinship with God's
creatures in the new creation" ("Wilderness and Paradise," 89).

[46] Conjectures, 131-32; see also 22, 34, 206, 234, 295.

[47] Ibid., 266.

[48] Ibid., 295.

[49] "Hagia Sophia," 506.

[50] On this see Woodcock, 151. On the dance, see Lipski, 48.

[51] Cf. an early reaction to Gethsemani: "It stood on top of
a high rampart of a retaining wall that made it look like a prison
or a citadel" (Mountain, 331).

[52] Speaking of his mature writing, Sr Thérèse says that "when
one comes into the wide country of his ripened thought one is astounded
at its depth, its richness, and its comprehension" ("The Solitary,"
in Hart, Thomas Merton/Monk, 73: emphasis mine).

[53] "... le Paradis est, pour l'essentiel, notre entrée dans
la vie intime des Trois Personnes divines, ce qui nous rapproche de

tous les hommes appelés effectivement à la communion dans l'amour
de Dieu" (Miquel and Sagne, col. 201).

[54]See p. 162, above.

[55]"Room with a View: Thomas Merton and Flannery O'Connor,"
Katallagete 8.1 (Summer 1982), 6.

[56]In TS2 he had first written "paradise," then crossed it out
and replaced it with "promised land"--in any case, an equivalent
image.

[57]Not profession, which took place in 1947.

[58]On the day after his final vows, he wrote in his journal:
"I am part of Gethsemani. I belong to the family. It is a family
about which I have no illusions. And the most satisfying thing
about this sense of incorporation is that I am glad to belong to
this community, not another ..." (Jonas, 40).

[59]See on this Labrie, 57-67.

[60]Woodcock, 107.

[61]Zen, 132.

[62]The phrase is a recurrent one in Merton; it occurs, for example, in a very significant dream in Conjectures (189, see also 150,
and cf. V 33, TS1).

[63]On epektasis (the spelling epektesis is sometimes seen),
see Bamberger, "The Monk," 37-38.

[64]Cameron-Brown, 166.

[65]The "Publisher's Note to New Edition" in a British reprint
of New Seeds reads: "At the author's request the word NEW is deleted
from the title of this work. The original Seeds of Contemplation
is now out of print but this present book retains the full substance of the earlier work and almost every chapter has been extended. There are also many additional chapters"--Seeds of Contemplation, Originally Published as New Seeds of Contemplation (Wheat-
hampstead, Hertfordshire, UK: Anthony Clarke Books, 1972), p. vii.
I find this very hard to believe, not least because the author had
died four years before publication. Even if it is correct (see
Robert E. Daggy's comment on "Merton's chronic vagueness about
foreign rights"--Introductions, 63), it is seriously misleading.
Seeds itself (whether SC or SCR, I do not know) has also been re-

printed without any comment in the book itself as to its place in
Merton's development (Westport, CT: Greenwood Press, 1979).

[66] "The Catholicizing of Contemplation," 189.

SELECT BIBLIOGRAPHY

This bibliography includes only those works of Merton cited in the text or notes. For other bibliographical resources, see the books mentioned in Ch. 1, n. 3, or the later bibliography in Richard A. Cashen, Solitude in the Thought of Thomas Merton (Kalamazoo: Cistercian Publications, 1981), 181-201.

Published Works

1948   The Seven Storey Mountain. New York: Harcourt, Brace.
        What is Contemplation? Springfield, IL: Templegate [1978].

1949   Seeds of Contemplation. Norfolk, CT: New Directions.
        Seeds of Contemplation, rev. ed. Norfolk, CT: New Directions.
        The Waters of Siloe. New York: Harcourt, Brace.

1950   Seeds of Contemplation, British rev. ed. London: Hollis
            and Carter.
        "Todo y Nada: Writing and Contemplation." Introd. Thérèse
            Lentfoehr. Renascence 2.2 (Spring 1950), 87-101.

1953   The Sign of Jonas. Garden City, NY: Doubleday [1956].

1955   No Man Is An Island. Garden City: Doubleday [1967].

1959   The Secular Journal of Thomas Merton. Garden City: Double-
            day [1969].

1960   Disputed Questions. Toronto: New American Library of
            Canada [1965].

1961   The New Man. London: Burns, Oates [1976].
        "The Recovery of Paradise," in James Laughlin, ed.,
            New Directions in Prose and Poetry 17. New York:
            New Directions, 81-101. Rpt. in A Thomas Merton Reader,
            rev. ed. (see below), 481-88; and in Zen and the Birds
            of Appetite (see below), 116-33.

1962   New Seeds of Contemplation. New York: New Directions [1972].
        A Thomas Merton Reader, rev. ed. Ed. Thomas P. McDonnell.
            Garden City: Doubleday, 1974.

1964   "The Humanity of Christ in Monastic Prayer." Monastic
            Studies 2, 1-27.

1966   Conjectures of a Guilty Bystander. Garden City: Doubleday
            [1968].

1967   Mystics and Zen Masters. New York: Delta [1969].
        "Wilderness and Paradise: Two Recent Studies." Cistercian
            Studies 2, 83-89.

1968   Faith and Violence: Christian Teaching and Christian Prac-
            tice. Notre Dame, IN: Notre Dame University Press.
        Zen and the Birds of Appetite. New York: New Directions.
        "Blake and the New Theology." Sewanee Review 76, 673-82.

1969   Contemplative Prayer. Garden City: Doubleday [1973].
        Introduction to Amédée Hallier, The Monastic Theology of
            Aelred of Rievaulx. Trans. Columban Heaney and Hugh
            McCaffery. Spencer, MA: Cistercian Publications, pp.
            vii-xiii.

1971   Contemplation in a World of Action. Introd. Jean Leclercq.
            Garden City: Doubleday [1973].
        Thomas Merton on Peace. Ed. and introd. Gordon Zahn. New
            York: McCall. Rpt. as The Nonviolent Alternative. New
            York: Farrar, Straus and Giroux, 1980.

1973   The Asian Journal of Thomas Merton. Ed. Naomi Burton,
            Patrick Hart and James Laughlin, consulting ed. Amiya
            Chakravarty. New York: New Directions.

1981   Introductions East & West. Ed. Robert E. Daggy. Greensboro,
            NC: Unicorn.

        [Dates in brackets are those of the edition used for this
            study if other than that of the original publication.]

Unpublished Items

[1947 or 1948]   Seeds of Contemplation (TS1). One hundred twenty-
                      six sheets.

[1948]   Memento Dei Genitrix (TS1a). MS of hymn printed
                      at the beginning of Seeds and Seeds Revised.

1949   Letter to Sr Thérèse Lentfoehr (May 13).

1960   Letter to Sr Thérèse Lentfoehr (December 5).

1961   New Seeds of Contemplation, insertions (TS2).
                    Eighty leaves, comprising 89 pages of text.

[n.d.]   "Seeds of Contemplation (1949)." Xerox of page
                    referring to Seeds in the catalogue of Merton
                    MSS and TSS then in the possession of Sr
                    Thérèse Lentfoehr and now at Columbia Uni-
                    versity; includes Merton's comment on the
                    missing notebooks containing the original
                    version of Seeds.

A NOTE ON READING MERTON

A very large number of people have told me that they began with great interest to read The Seven Storey Mountain and gave up part way through in disgust at the smugness of the author as he then was. If you have had this experience, or if you are just beginning to read Merton, may I make these suggestions?

First, read something short to give yourself a sense of the overall shape of his life, such as Herbert O'Driscoll's prologue ("Hermitage of a Thousand Windows") in Donald Grayston and Michael W. Higgins, Thomas Merton: Pilgrim in Process (Toronto: Griffin House, 1983), pp. xv-xxxviii. Then read his major autobiographical works in order: the Mountain, Jonas, Conjectures and the Asian Journal. Don't try to understand or remember the myriad names and allusions and references to other works that you will find in these books: just let them all wash over or through you. Then go on to Seeds, the first edition, and New Seeds, read separately, perhaps with a few days' interval, in order to get the feel of the earlier and later Merton in a clear way. Finally, dip into A Thomas Merton Reader, in the revised edition of 1974, to obtain some idea of the breadth of his interests.

With just that much preparatory reading, you will be able to contextualize Merton's other writings, assess the judgements of scholars and critics in the secondary literature on Merton, and go on from his writings to your own exploration of his great concerns: contemplation, peace and nonviolence, and the encounter in transforming depth, in our age, of the world's great faith-traditions.

Sit finis libri, non finis quaerendi--"it may be the end of the book; it is not the end of the searching" (Mountain, 423). The epigraph Merton chose for the Mountain can continue to serve us all very well as our own reading and searching continues.

INDEX

TORONTO STUDIES IN THEOLOGY